Simple Psalter

for Year C

J. Michael Joncas

LITURGICAL PRESS
Collegeville, Minnesota

litpress.org

ACKNOWLEDGMENTS

Cover design: Tara Wiese. Photo courtesy of Getty Images.

The English translation of Psalm Responses from *Lectionary for Mass* © 1969, 1981, 1997, International Commission on English in the Liturgy Corporation. All rights reserved.

Verse texts from *The Abbey Psalms and Canticles* by the Monks of Conception Abbey, © 2018, 2010, United States Conference of Catholic Bishops. All rights reserved.

© 2024 The Jan Michael Joncas Trust.
Published by Liturgical Press, Collegeville, Minnesota. All rights reserved. No part of this book may be used or reproduced in any manner whatsoever except brief quotations in reviews, without the written permission of Liturgical Press, Saint John's Abbey, PO Box 7500, Collegeville, MN 56321-7500. Printed in the United States of America.

ISBN: 978-0-8146-6787-3 ISBN: 978-0-8146-6788-0 (e-book)

Contents

Psalms for feast days and solemnities, such as Christmas and Easter, can be found in *Simple Psalter for Solemnities, Feasts, and Other Celebrations*. Available at litpress.org.

First Sunday of Advent (Psalm 25: To You, O Lord, I Lift My Soul) 8

Second Sunday of Advent (Psalm 126: The Lord Has Done Great Things) 12

Third Sunday of Advent (Isaiah 12: Cry Out with Joy and Gladness) 16

Fourth Sunday of Advent (Psalm 80: Lord, Make Us Turn to You) 20

First Sunday of Lent (Psalm 91: Be with Me, Lord) 24

Second Sunday of Lent (Psalm 27: The Lord Is My Light) 28

Third Sunday of Lent (Psalm 103: The Lord Is Kind) 32

Fourth Sunday of Lent (Psalm 34: Taste and See) 36

Fifth Sunday of Lent (Psalm 126: The Lord Has Done Great Things) 40

Second Sunday of Easter / Sunday of Divine Mercy (Psalm 118: Give Thanks to the Lord) 44

Third Sunday of Easter (Psalm 30: I Will Praise You, Lord) 48

Fourth Sunday of Easter (Psalm 100: We Are His People) 52

Fifth Sunday of Easter (Psalm 145: I Will Praise Your Name for Ever) 56

Sixth Sunday of Easter (Psalm 67: O God, Let All the Nations Praise You) 60

Seventh Sunday of Easter (Psalm 97: The Lord Is King) 64

Solemnity of the Most Holy Trinity (Psalm 8: O Lord, Our God, How Wonderful Your Name) 68

Solemnity of the Body and Blood of Christ (Psalm 110: You Are a Priest for Ever) 72

Second Sunday in Ordinary Time (Psalm 96: Proclaim His Marvelous Deeds) 76

Third Sunday in Ordinary Time (Psalm 19: Your Words, O Lord) 80

Fourth Sunday in Ordinary Time (Psalm 71: I Will Sing of Your Salvation) 84

Fifth Sunday in Ordinary Time (Psalm 138: In the Sight of the Angels) 88

Sixth Sunday in Ordinary Time (Psalm 1: Blessed Are They) 92

Seventh Sunday in Ordinary Time (Psalm 103: The Lord Is Kind) 96

Eighth Sunday in Ordinary Time (Psalm 92: Lord, It Is Good) 100

Ninth Sunday in Ordinary Time (Psalm 117: Go Out to All the World) 104

Tenth Sunday in Ordinary Time (Psalm 30: I Will Praise You, Lord) 106

Eleventh Sunday in Ordinary Time (Psalm 32: Lord, Forgive the Wrong) 110

Twelfth Sunday in Ordinary Time (Psalm 63: My Soul Is Thirsting for You) 114

Thirteenth Sunday in Ordinary Time (Psalm 16: You Are My Inheritance) 118

Fourteenth Sunday in Ordinary Time (Psalm 66: Let All the Earth) 122

Fifteenth Sunday in Ordinary Time, first setting (Psalm 69: Turn to the Lord) 126

Fifteenth Sunday in Ordinary Time, second setting (Psalm 19: Lord, You Have the Words) 130

Sixteenth Sunday in Ordinary Time (Psalm 15: The One Who Does Justice) 134

Seventeenth Sunday in Ordinary Time (Psalm 138: Lord, on the Day I Called for Help) 138

Eighteenth Sunday in Ordinary Time (Psalm 90: If Today You Hear His Voice) 142

Nineteenth Sunday in Ordinary Time (Psalm 33: Blessed the People) 147

Twentieth Sunday in Ordinary Time (Psalm 40: Lord, Come to My Aid) 150

Twenty-First Sunday in Ordinary Time (Psalm 117: Go Out to All the World) 154

Twenty-Second Sunday in Ordinary Time (Psalm 68: God in Your Goodness) 156

Twenty-Third Sunday in Ordinary Time (Psalm 90: In Every Age, O Lord) 160

Twenty-Fourth Sunday in Ordinary Time (Psalm 51: I Will Rise) 164

Twenty-Fifth Sunday in Ordinary Time (Psalm 113: Praise the Lord) 168

Twenty-Sixth Sunday in Ordinary Time (Psalm 146: Praise the Lord, My Soul!) 172

Twenty-Seventh Sunday in Ordinary Time (Psalm 95: If Today You Hear His Voice) 176

Twenty-Eighth Sunday in Ordinary Time (Psalm 98: The Lord Has Revealed) 180

Twenty-Ninth Sunday in Ordinary Time (Psalm 121: Our Help Is from the Lord) 184

Thirtieth Sunday in Ordinary Time (Psalm 34: The Lord Hears the Cry) 188

Thirty-First Sunday in Ordinary Time (Psalm 145: I Will Praise Your Name for Ever) 192

Thirty-Second Sunday in Ordinary Time (Psalm 17: Lord, When Your Glory Appears) 196

Thirty-Third Sunday in Ordinary Time (Psalm 98: The Lord Comes to Rule the Earth) 200

Solemnity of Christ the King / Thirty-Fourth Sunday in Ordinary Time
(Psalm 122: Let Us Go Rejoicing) 204

Composer's Notes

My "simple psalms" project is intended to help worshiping communities with limited musical resources to sing the appointed Responsorial Psalm for the Sundays and Holydays of the Liturgical Year. I have set the texts as they appear in the English-language *Lectionary for Mass, Second Typical Edition* (1998) (antiphons) and the *Abbey Psalms and Canticles* (verses). All of the antiphons are set metrically (i.e., not in the free rhythm of chant) because I believe that in most cases in the English-speaking world this makes their texts more memorable and easier to sing for the assembly. The verses are set to rhythmic psalm-tones similar to those of Gelineau psalmody (i.e., speech-rhythm settings of the text over pulsed accompaniment ["sprung rhythm"]). Unlike the published Gelineau psalms, however, I have notated the way I propose that the texts to be sung since I find that it is sometimes difficult for cantors to sing the Gelineau tones as notated using only whole notes. A suggested tempo appears at the beginning of each psalm as a metronome mark; this tempo can be adjusted depending on the acoustic properties of the space in which the liturgy is celebrated.

Tones are assigned to each psalm based on the genre (*Gattung*) of the psalm-text, following the pattern of my friend and colleague, Art Zannoni, as follows:

Tone 1A: Hymn of Praise, Motivation from Nature

Tone 1B: Hymn of Praise, Motivation from History or Torah

Tone 1C: Song of Zion

Tone 1D: Processional

Tone 1E: Hymn of Praise to YHWH as King

Tone 2A: Royal Coronation or Anniversary

Tone 2C: Royal Song of Thanksgiving

Tone 2D: Royal Marriage Song

Tone 3: Prophetic Psalm

Tone 4A: Community Lament

Tone 4B: Individual Lament

Tone 4C: Prayer for the Sick

Tone 5A: Communal Thanksgiving

Tone 5B: Individual Thanksgiving

Tone 6: Psalm of Confidence

Tone 8A: Wisdom Psalm 1

Tone 8B: Wisdom Psalm 2

(Missing tone numbers indicate a psalm-genre that does not appear in the Sunday and Solemnity Lectionary.)

I would here like to acknowledge the influence of three church composers whose psalm settings have influenced this project. I have already mentioned Fr. Joseph Gelineau, S.J., whose groundbreaking creation of "pulsed" psalm-tones set to sprung-rhythm texts made one of the metrical characteristics of Hebrew biblical psalms and canticles available for vernacular singing. A second influence was Howard Hughes, S.M., whose assigning of particular tones to particular genres of psalms based in contemporary form-critical analysis of the psalm-texts, has been eye- and ear-opening for me. Finally Paul Inwood was the first to call my attention to the idea of "psalm tunes" (rather than "psalm tones"). He showed how many English-language folk songs adjusted the fundamental melodic curves of their tones, eliding some syllables while assigning multiple notes to a single syllable based on the number of syllables needed.

Following the practice articulated in the *Lectionary for Mass*, these Responsorial Psalms would be performed as follows. After a period of silence to reflect on the previous scriptural reading proclaimed, a keyboard (or melody instrument) would play the melody for the Antiphon alone. The cantor would immediately intone the Antiphon with a keyboard providing accompaniment, if needed. The assembly would then repeat the Antiphon with a keyboard (and optionally other instruments) providing accompaniment, if needed. The cantor would then sing the assigned psalm verses with the assembly repeating the Antiphon after each verse.

While I believe these "simple psalms" can effectively be sung *a cappella* or with simple keyboard accompaniment, some communities might want to enhance their singing of the Responsorial Psalm with more elaborate music.

The optional harmony additions to the antiphons can be performed in a multitude of ways.

Vocally, the harmonies:

1) might be sung by soloists with the rest of the choir singing the antiphon in unison with the assembly.

2) might be sung by the soprano and alto sections of the choir with the men singing the antiphon in unison with the assembly.

3) If an SATB texture is desired, the soprano and bass sections sing the antiphon in unison with the assembly, with the tenors singing the higher harmonies an octave lower than written and the altos singing the lower harmonies as notated.

Instrumentally,

1) the SA harmonies might be played by C treble wind or string instruments, either as notated or an octave higher depending on where it best fits the instruments' tessitura.

2) the keyboardist should keep the pulse constant under the singing of the verses, but might repeat the chords as quarter notes rather than half notes, or even arpeggiate the chords as eighth notes if desired.

My preference is that the Verses be sung by a solo cantorial voice since that seems to ensure that the psalm-text be clearly sung and understood. Most of the time I have set the psalm-text for two phrases on one breath; the cantor should feel free to take a breath at an appropriate place if singing both phrases on one breath is too taxing. It is also possible to alternate male and female solo voices on the Verses, possibly with both singing the final Verse in octaves. It would also be possible to have the choir sing the verses (or just the final Verse) in unison, as long as their articulation keeps the psalm-text intelligible.

As the *Lectionary for Mass* reminds us: "The working of the Holy Spirit is needed if the word of God is to make what we hear outwardly have its effect inwardly. Because of the Holy Spirit's inspiration and support, the word of God becomes the foundation of the liturgical celebration and the rule and support of all our life. The working of the Holy Spirit precedes, accompanies and brings to completion the whole celebration of the Liturgy. But the Spirit also brings home to each person individually everything that in the proclamation of the word of God is spoken for the good of the whole gathering of the faithful" [9]. I pray that my musical settings of these "simple psalms" may help Christ's faithful, individually and collectively, hear the word of God and put it into practice in their lives. *Soli Deo gloria*.

(Fr. Jan) Michael Joncas
St. Paul, MN

Psalm 25: To You, O Lord, I Lift My Soul
First Sunday of Advent, Year C

Ps 25:4-5, 8-9, 10 and 14

Michael Joncas
Tone 6: Psalm of Confidence

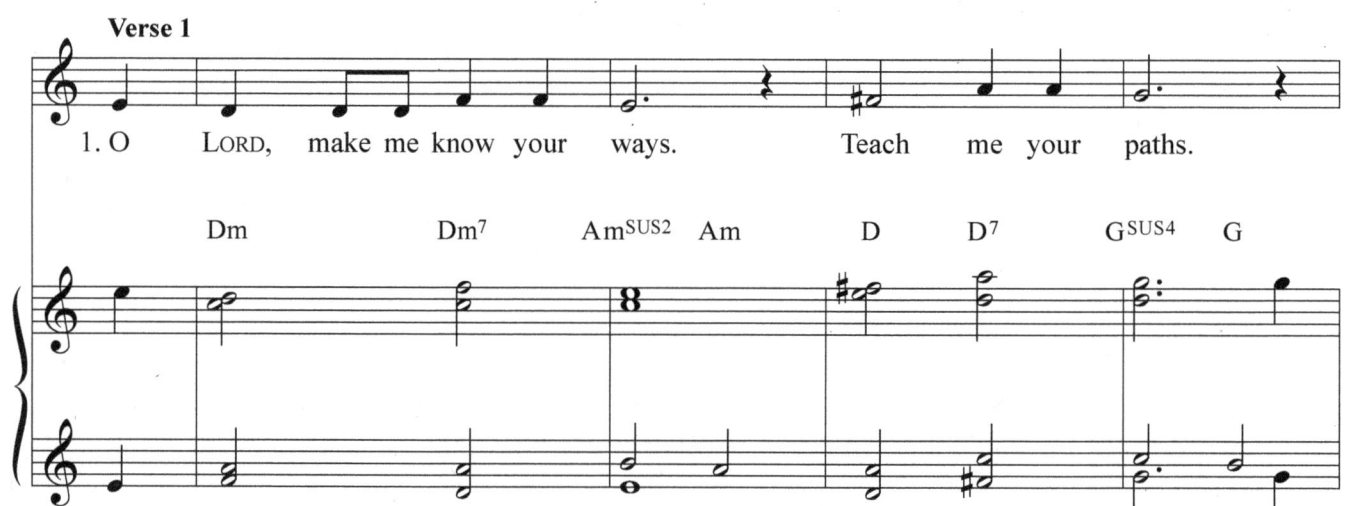

First Sunday of Advent, Year C

First Sunday of Advent, Year C

Psalm 126: The Lord Has Done Great Things
Second Sunday of Advent, Year C

Ps 126:1-2ab, 2cd-3, 4-5, 6

Michael Joncas
Tone 1B: Hymn of Praise, Motivation from History or Torah

Second Sunday of Advent, Year C

Second Sunday of Advent, Year C

Second Sunday of Advent, Year C

Verse 4

4. They go out, they go out, full of tears, bear-ing seed for the sow-ing; they come

(D)   (C/D)   (Bm) (D)   (Em) (D)   (A SUS4) (A)
F   Eb/F   Dm   F   Gm   F   C SUS4   C

back, they come back with a song, bear - ing their sheaves.

(Am)   (Cmaj7)   (D SUS2)   (D)   (Am)   (Am7)   (D SUS4)   (D)
Cm   Ebmaj7   F SUS2   F   Cm   Cm7   F SUS4   F

Ant.

Isaiah 12: Cry Out with Joy and Gladness
Third Sunday of Advent, Year C

Is 12:2-3, 4bcd, 5-6

Michael Joncas

Third Sunday of Advent, Year C

Third Sunday of Advent, Year C

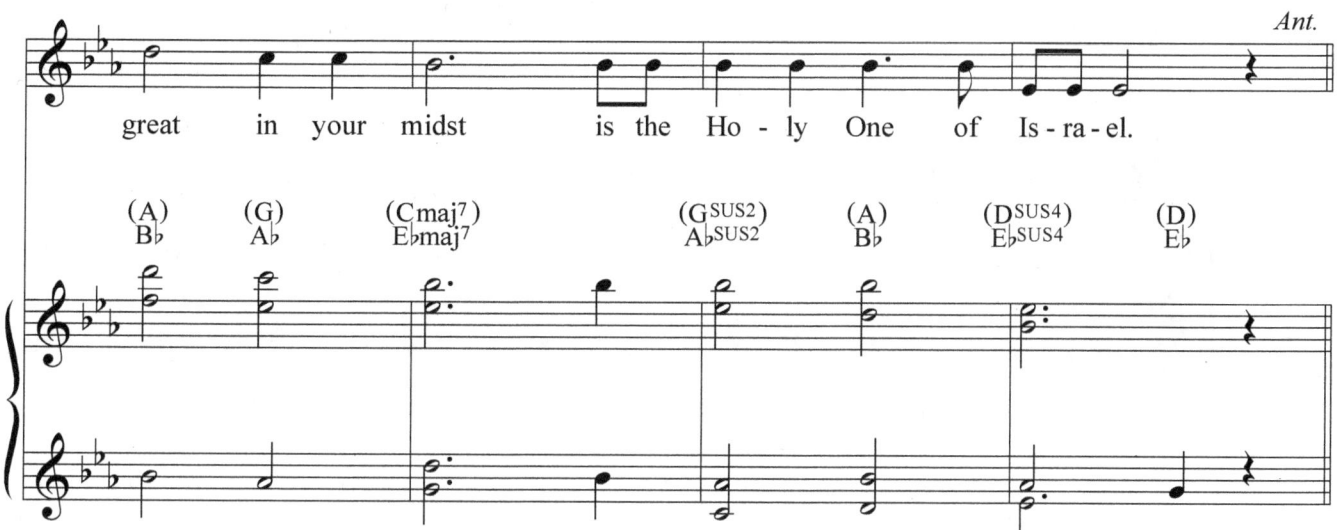

Ant.

great in your midst is the Ho - ly One of Is - ra - el.

Psalm 80: Lord, Make Us Turn to You
Fourth Sunday of Advent, Year C

Ps 80:2ac and 3b, 15-16, 18-19

Michael Joncas
Tone 4A: Community Lament

Fourth Sunday of Advent, Year C

Fourth Sunday of Advent, Year C

Fourth Sunday of Advent, Year C

Psalm 91: Be with Me, Lord
First Sunday of Lent, Year C

Ps 91:1-2, 10-11, 12-13, 14-15

Michael Joncas
Tone 6: Psalm of Confidence

Text: Refrain, *Lectionary for Mass*, © 1969, 1997, ICEL;
Verses, *The Abbey Psalms and Canticles*, © 2010, 2018, United States Conference of Catholic Bishops, Washington, DC. All rights reserved.
Music: copyright © 2024 The Jan Michael Joncas Trust. Published and administered by Liturgical Press, Collegeville, MN 56321. All rights reserved.

First Sunday of Lent, Year C

First Sunday of Lent, Year C

Verse 3

3. They shall bear you up-on their hands, lest you strike your foot a-gainst a stone. On the

li-on and the vi - per you will tread, and tram-ple the young li - on and the ser - pent.

Verse 4

4. Since he clings to me in love, I will free him, pro - tect him, for he knows my

First Sunday of Lent, Year C

Psalm 27: The Lord Is My Light
Second Sunday of Lent, Year C

Ps 27: 1, 7-8ab, **8c-9abcd***,13-14

Michael Joncas
Tone 6: Psalm of Confidence

*NB: USCCB has an incorrect verse reference. The *Ordo Lectionum Missae* gives 8c-9abc only (**not** 9d) as in other national lectionaries.

Second Sunday of Lent, Year C

Second Sunday of Lent, Year C

Second Sunday of Lent, Year C

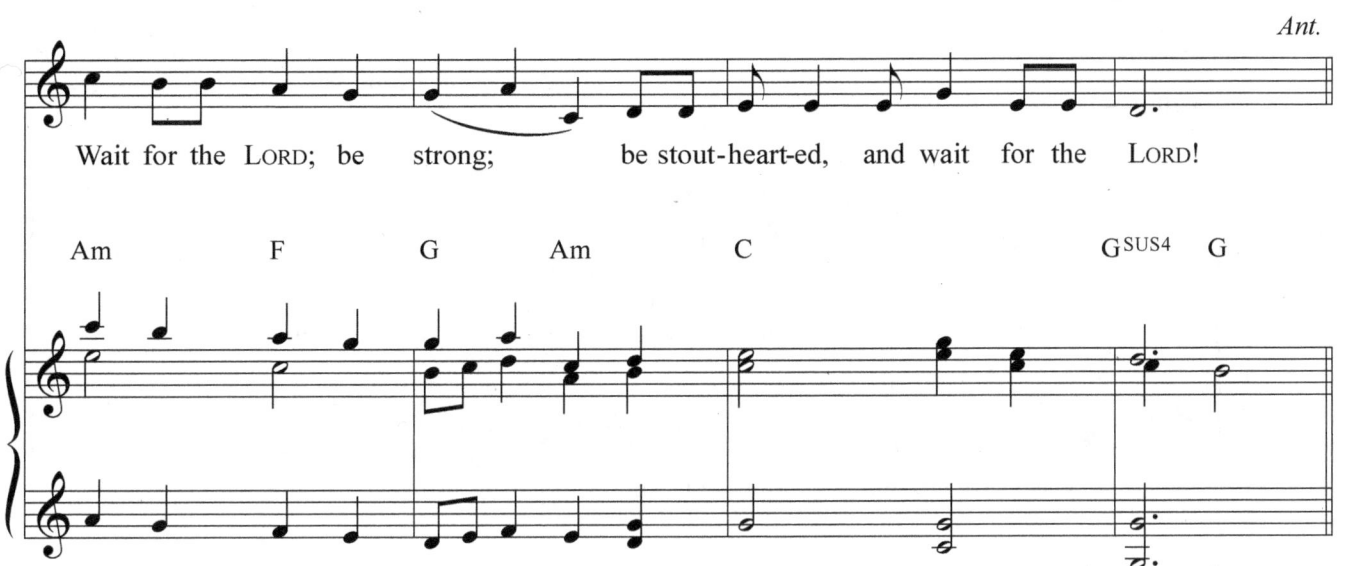

Psalm 103: The Lord Is Kind
Third Sunday of Lent, Year C

Ps 103:1-2, 3-4, 6-7, 8 and 11

Michael Joncas
Tone 5B: Individual Thanksgiving

Third Sunday of Lent, Year C

Third Sunday of Lent, Year C

Psalm 34: Taste and See
Fourth Sunday of Lent, Year C

Ps 34:2-3, 4-5, 6-7

Michael Joncas
Tone 8A: Wisdom Psalm 1

Fourth Sunday of Lent, Year C

Fourth Sunday of Lent, Year C

Psalm 126: The Lord Has Done Great Things
Fifth Sunday of Lent, Year C

Ps 126:1-2ab, 2cd-3, 4-5, 6

Michael Joncas
Tone 1B: Hymn of Praise, Motivation from History or Torah

Fifth Sunday of Lent, Year C

Fifth Sunday of Lent, Year C

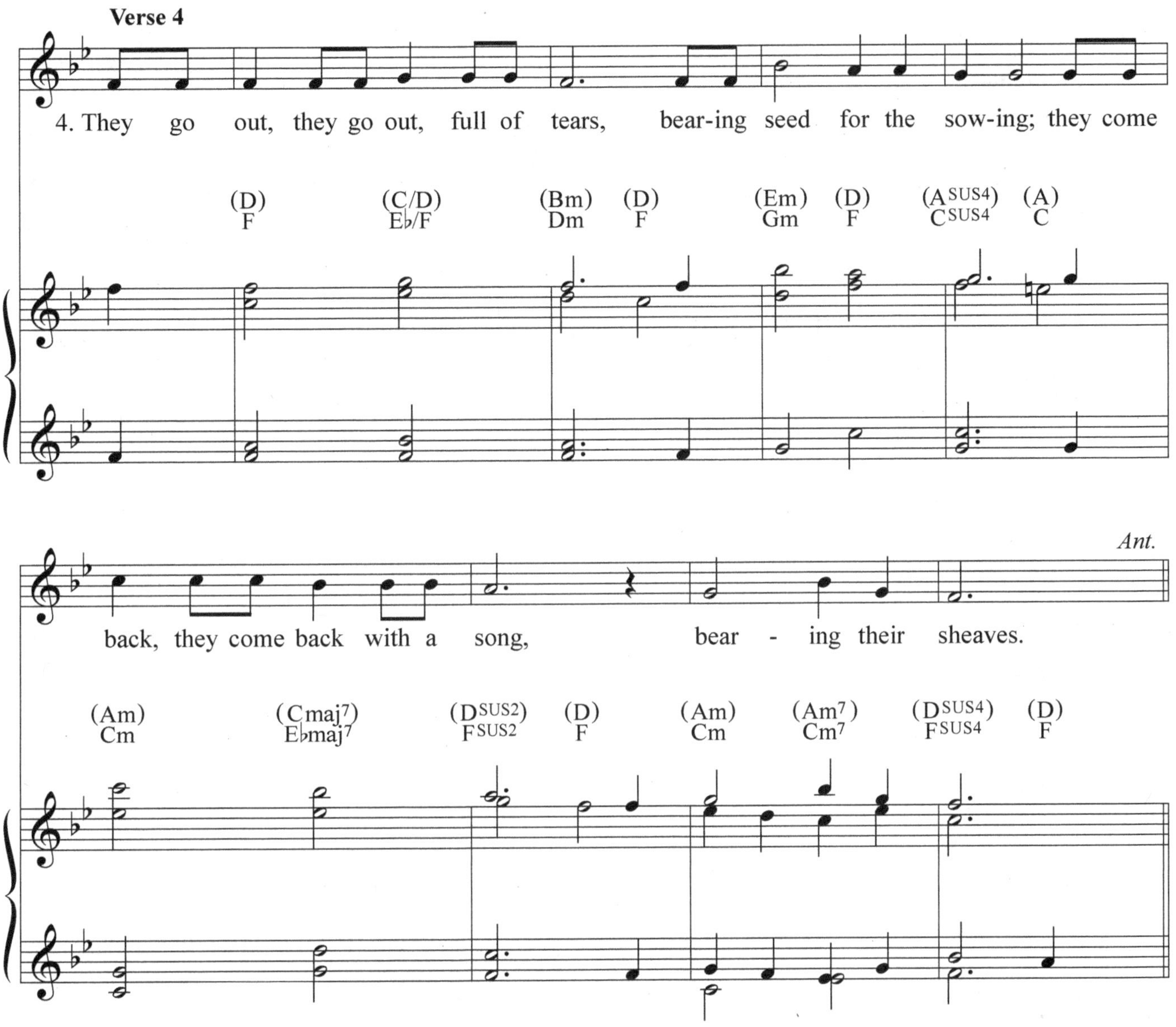
Verse 4
4. They go out, they go out, full of tears, bear-ing seed for the sow-ing; they come
(D) F (C/D) E♭/F (Bm) Dm (D) F (Em) Gm (D) F (ASUS4) CSUS4 (A) C
Ant.
back, they come back with a song, bear - ing their sheaves.
(Am) Cm (Cmaj7) E♭maj7 (DSUS2) FSUS2 (D) F (Am) Cm (Am7) Cm7 (DSUS4) FSUS4 (D) F

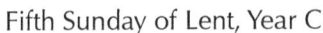

Psalm 118: Give Thanks to the Lord
Second Sunday of Easter/Sunday of Divine Mercy, Years A, B, and C

Ps 118:1-2, 16-17, 22-23

Michael Joncas
Tone 5B: Individual Thanksgiving

Second Sunday of Easter/Sunday of Divine Mercy, Years A, B, and C

Second Sunday of Easter/Sunday of Divine Mercy, Years A, B, and C

Second Sunday of Easter/Sunday of Divine Mercy, Years A, B, and C

Psalm 30: I Will Praise You, Lord
Third Sunday of Easter, Year C

Ps 30:2, 4, 5-6, 11-12, 13

Michael Joncas
Tone 4C: Prayer for the Sick

Third Sunday of Easter, Year C

Third Sunday of Easter, Year C

Third Sunday of Easter, Year C

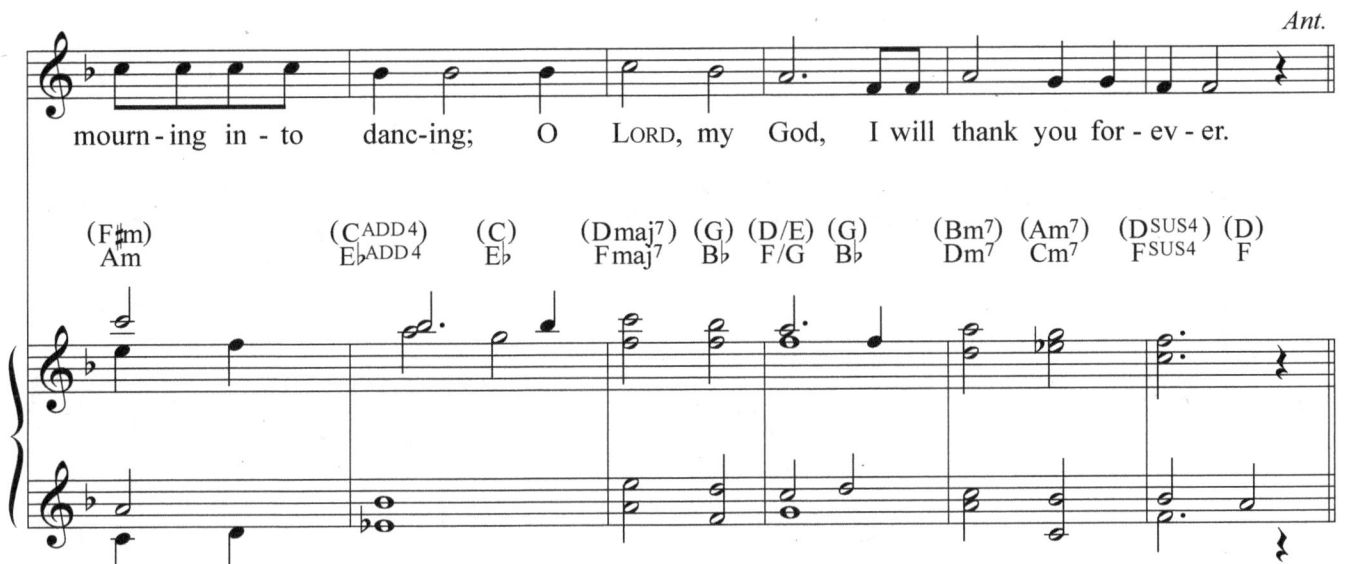

Psalm 100: We Are His People
Fourth Sunday of Easter, Year C

Ps 100:1-2, 3, 5

Michael Joncas
Tone 1D: Processional

Antiphon

March-like ♩ = 100

Harmony: We are his peo-ple, the sheep of his flock, the sheep of his

Melody: We are his peo-ple, the sheep of his flock, the sheep of his

C G⁷ C F Am G^SUS4 G Dm⁷ G

Alternate Antiphon

flock. Al - le-lu - ia, Al - le-lu - ia. Al - le-lu - ia,

flock. Al - le-lu - ia, Al - le-lu - ia. Al - le-lu - ia,

C C G⁷ C F Am G^SUS4 G

Fourth Sunday of Easter, Year C

Fourth Sunday of Easter, Year C

Fourth Sunday of Easter, Year C

Psalm 145: I Will Praise Your Name for Ever
Fifth Sunday of Easter, Year C

Ps 145:8-9, 10-11, 12-13ab

Michael Joncas
Tone 1B: Hymn of Praise,
Motivation from History or Torah

Fifth Sunday of Easter, Year C

Fifth Sunday of Easter, Year C

Fifth Sunday of Easter, Year C

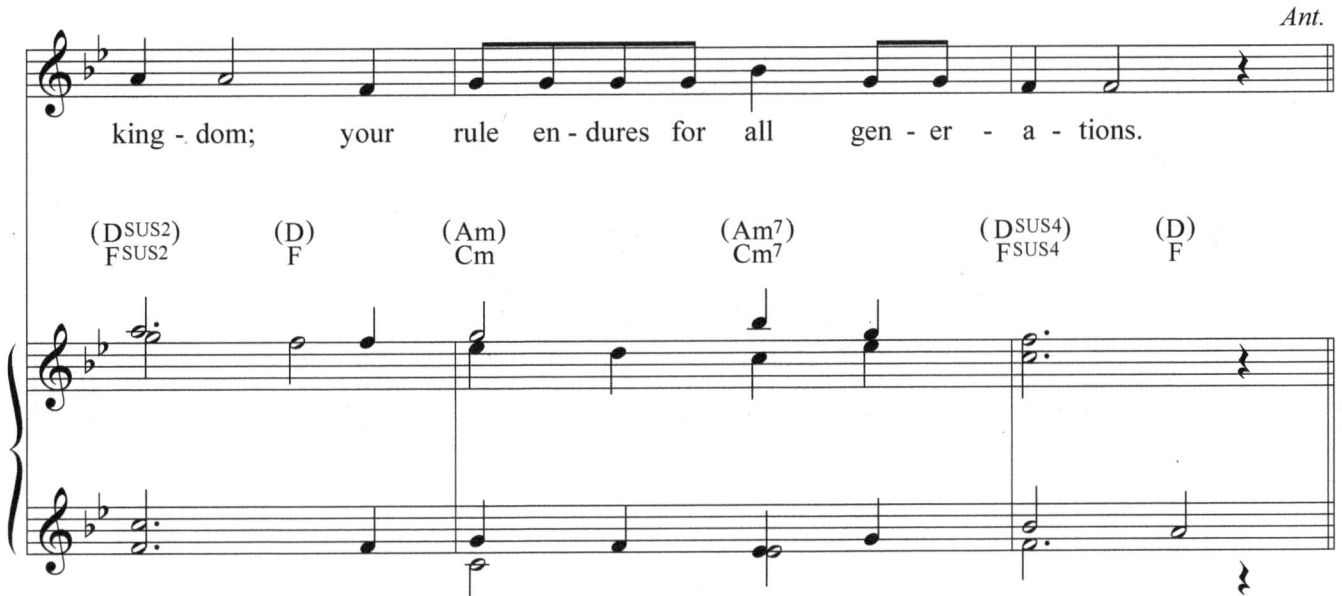

Psalm 67: O God, Let All the Nations Praise You

Sixth Sunday of Easter, Year C

Ps 67:2-3, 5, 6 and 8

Michael Joncas
Tone 5A: Communal Thanksgiving

Sixth Sunday of Easter, Year C

Sixth Sunday of Easter, Year C

Verse 2

2. Let the na-tions be glad and shout for joy; with up - right-ness you rule the peo-ples, you guide the na-tions on earth.

Verse 3

3. Let the peo - ples praise you, O God; let all the peo - ples

Sixth Sunday of Easter, Year C

Psalm 97: The Lord Is King
Seventh Sunday of Easter, Year C

Ps 97: 1 and 2b, 6 and 7c, 9

Michael Joncas
Tone 1E: Hymn of Praise to YHWH as King

Antiphon

With confidence ♩ = 80

Harmony

The Lord is king; the Lord is king, the most high o-ver all the earth.

Melody

The Lord is king; the Lord is king, the most high o-ver all the earth.

G   D   G   D   Em   Am⁷   D^SUS4   D   G

Alternate Antiphon

Al - le - lu - ia, al - le - lu - ia, al - le - lu - ia.

Al - le - lu - ia, al - le - lu - ia, al - le - lu - ia.

G   D   D   D   Em   Am⁷   D^SUS4   D   G

Seventh Sunday of Easter, Year C

Psalm 8: O Lord, Our God, How Wonderful Your Name
Solemnity of the Most Holy Trinity, Year C

Ps 8:4-5, 6-7, 8-9

Michael Joncas
Tone 1A: Hymn of Praise,
Motivation from Nature

Antiphon

With awe ♩ = 90

O Lord, our God, how won-der-ful your name, how won-der-ful your name, your name in all the earth!

Solemnity of the Most Holy Trinity, Year C

Solemnity of the Most Holy Trinity, Year C

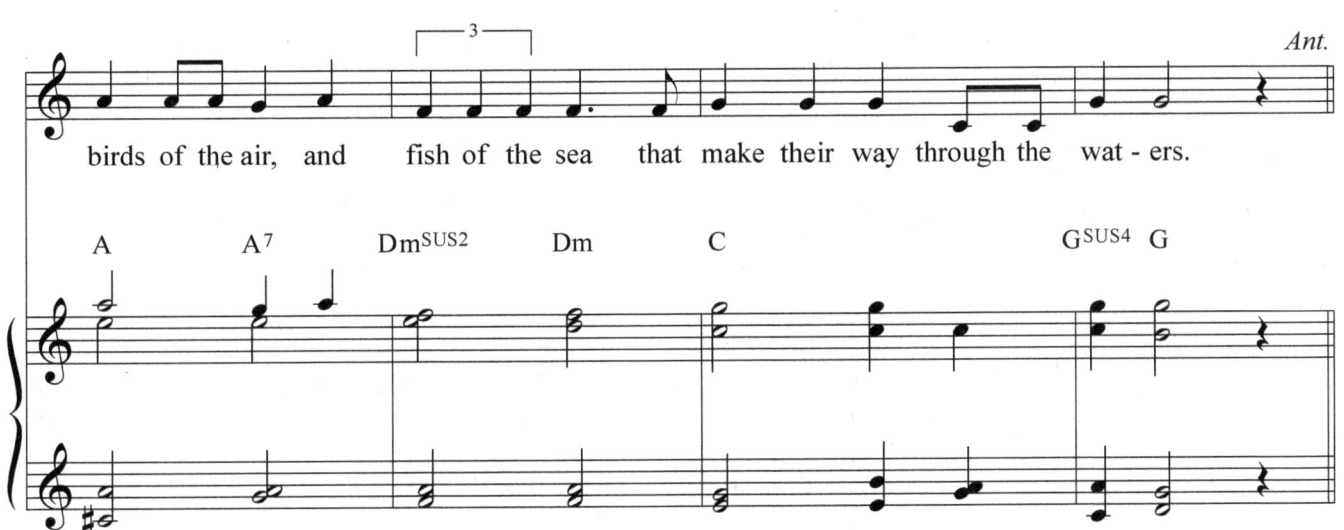

Psalm 110: You Are a Priest for Ever
Solemnity of the Body and Blood of Christ, Year C

Ps 110:1, 2, 3, 4

Michael Joncas
Tone 2A: Royal Coronation or Anniversary

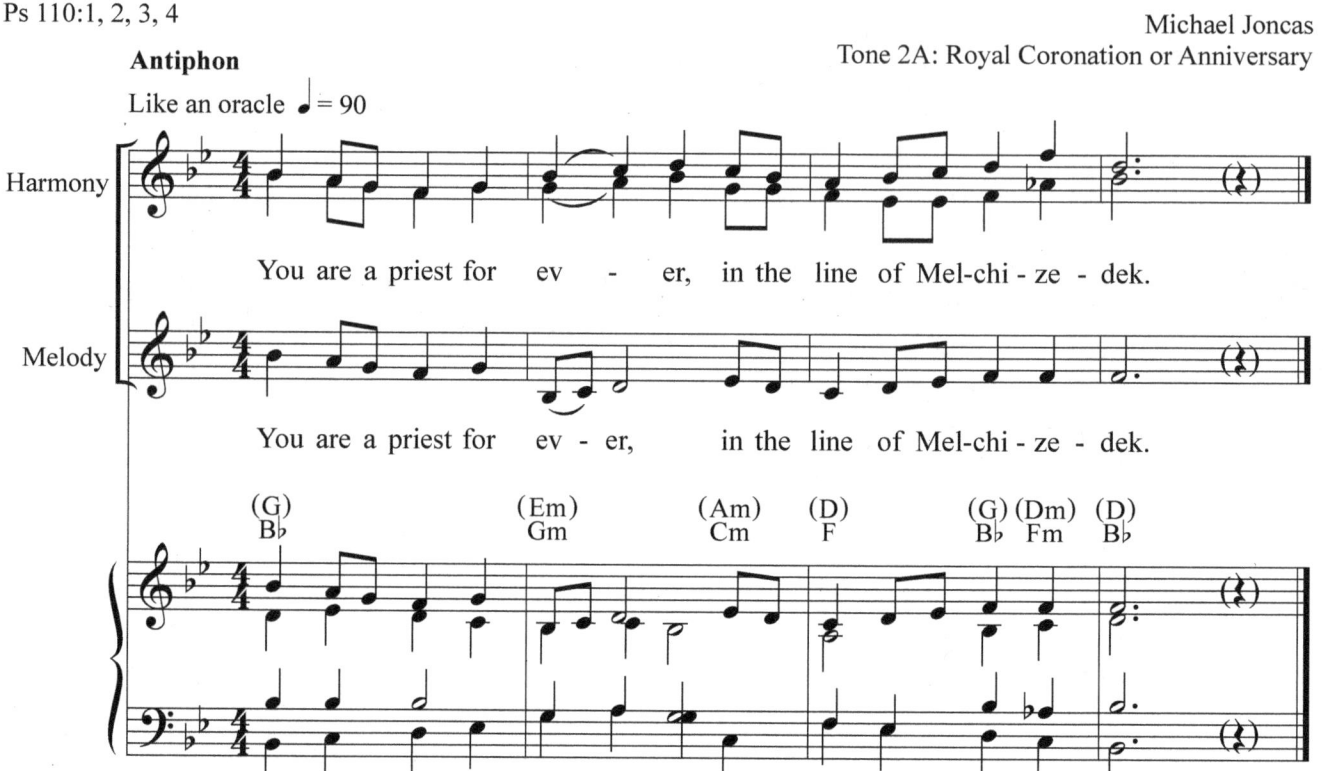

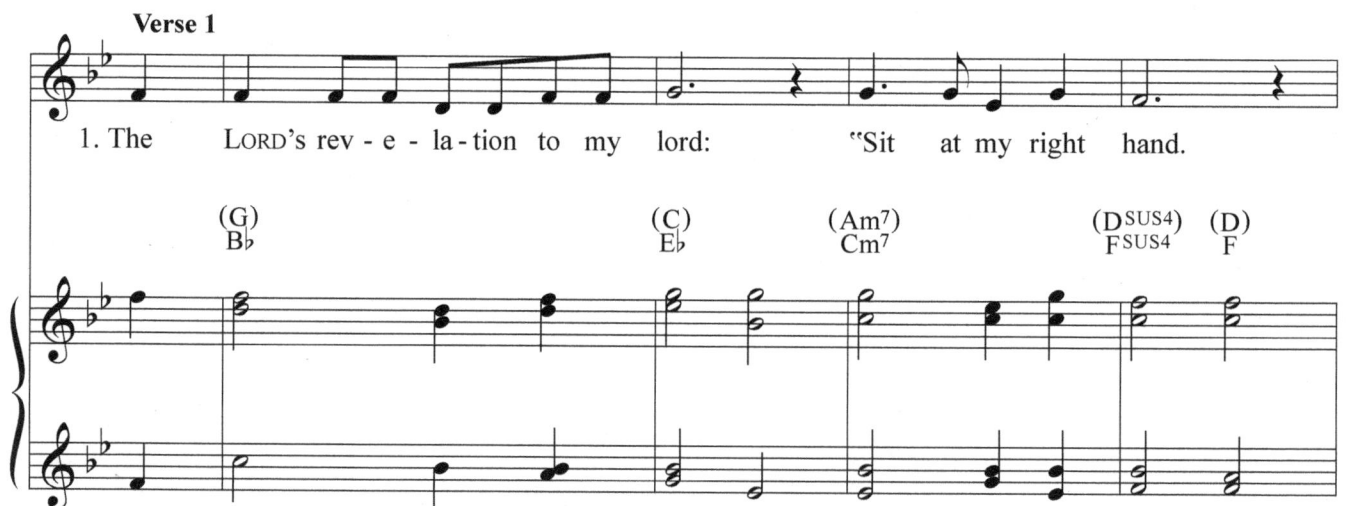

Solemnity of the Body and Blood of Christ, Year C

Solemnity of the Body and Blood of Christ, Year C

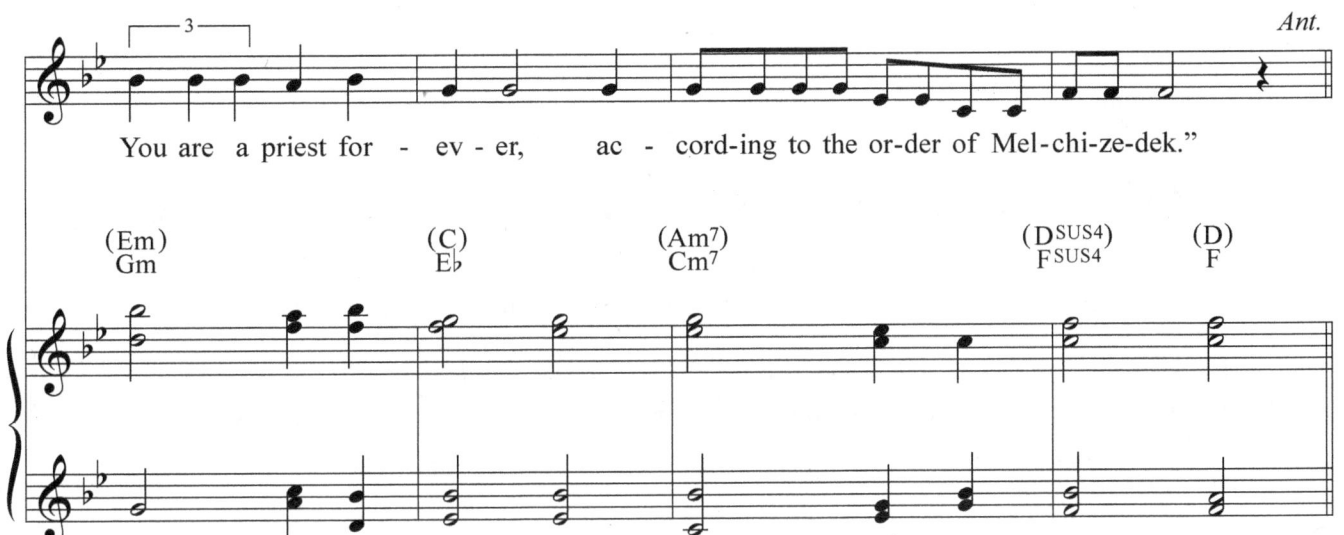

You are a priest for - ev - er, ac - cord-ing to the or-der of Mel-chi-ze-dek."

Psalm 96: Proclaim His Marvelous Deeds
Second Sunday in Ordinary Time, Year C

Ps 96:1-2a, 2b-3, 7-8a, 9-10ac

Michael Joncas
Tone 1E: Hymn of Praise to YHWH as King

Second Sunday in Ordinary Time, Year C

Second Sunday in Ordinary Time, Year C

Second Sunday in Ordinary Time, Year C

Psalm 19: Your Words, O Lord
Third Sunday in Ordinary Time, Year C

Ps 19:8, 9, 10, 15

Michael Joncas
Tone 8B: Wisdom Psalm 2

Third Sunday in Ordinary Time, Year C

Ant.

crees of the LORD are stead-fast; they give wis-dom to the sim-ple.

(Bm) (F♯m) (Gmaj⁷) (EmADD6) (Dmaj⁷) (G) (ASUS4) (A)
Cm Gm A♭maj⁷ FmADD6 E♭maj⁷ A♭ B♭SUS4 B♭

Verse 2

2. The pre-cepts of the LORD are right, they glad-den the heart. The com-

(D⁶) (G) (Em⁷) (A) (D⁶) (E⁷) (ASUS4) (A⁷/G)
E♭⁶ A♭ Fm⁷ B♭ E♭⁶ F⁷ B♭SUS4 B♭⁷/A♭

Ant.

mand of the LORD is clear; it gives light to the eyes.

(Bm) (F♯m) (Gmaj⁷) (EmADD6) (Dmaj⁷) (G) (ASUS4) (A)
Cm Gm A♭maj⁷ FmADD6 E♭maj⁷ A♭ B♭SUS4 B♭

Third Sunday in Ordinary Time, Year C

Verse 3

3. The fear of the LORD is pure, a - bid - ing for - ev - er. The

judg-ments of the LORD are true; they are, all of them, just.

Ant.

Verse 4

4. May the spo - ken words of my mouth, the thoughts of my heart, win

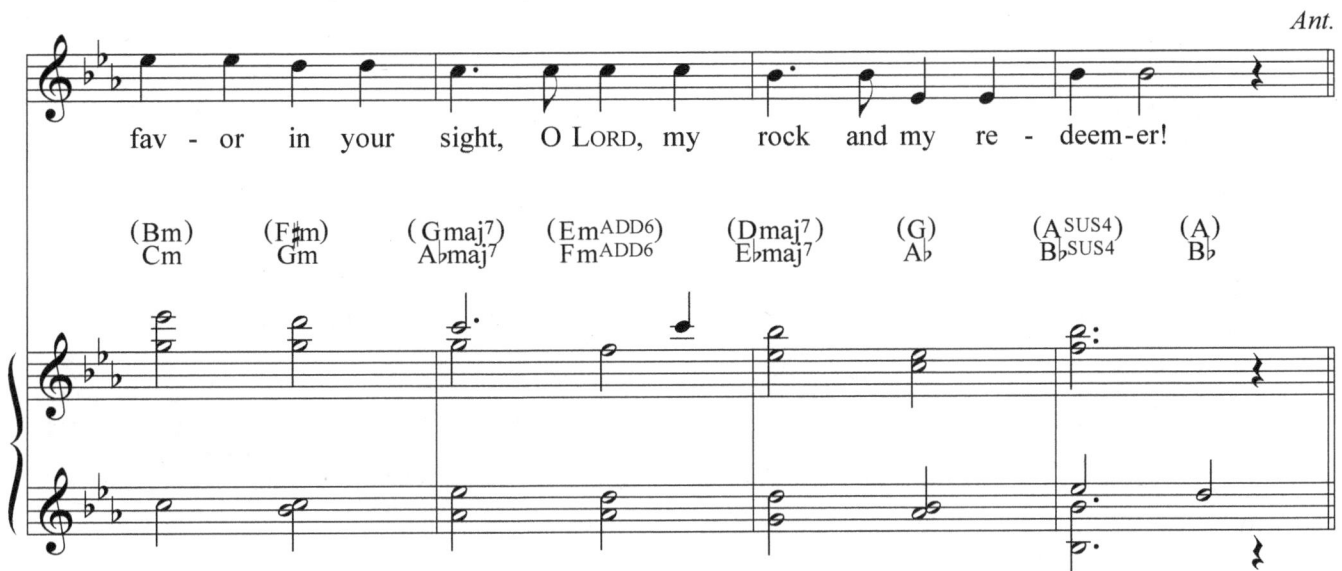

Psalm 71: I Will Sing of Your Salvation
Fourth Sunday in Ordinary Time, Year C

Ps 71:1-2, 3-4a, 5-6ab, 15ab and 17

Michael Joncas
Tone 4B: Individual Lament

Fourth Sunday in Ordinary Time, Year C

Fourth Sunday in Ordinary Time, Year C

Fourth Sunday in Ordinary Time, Year C

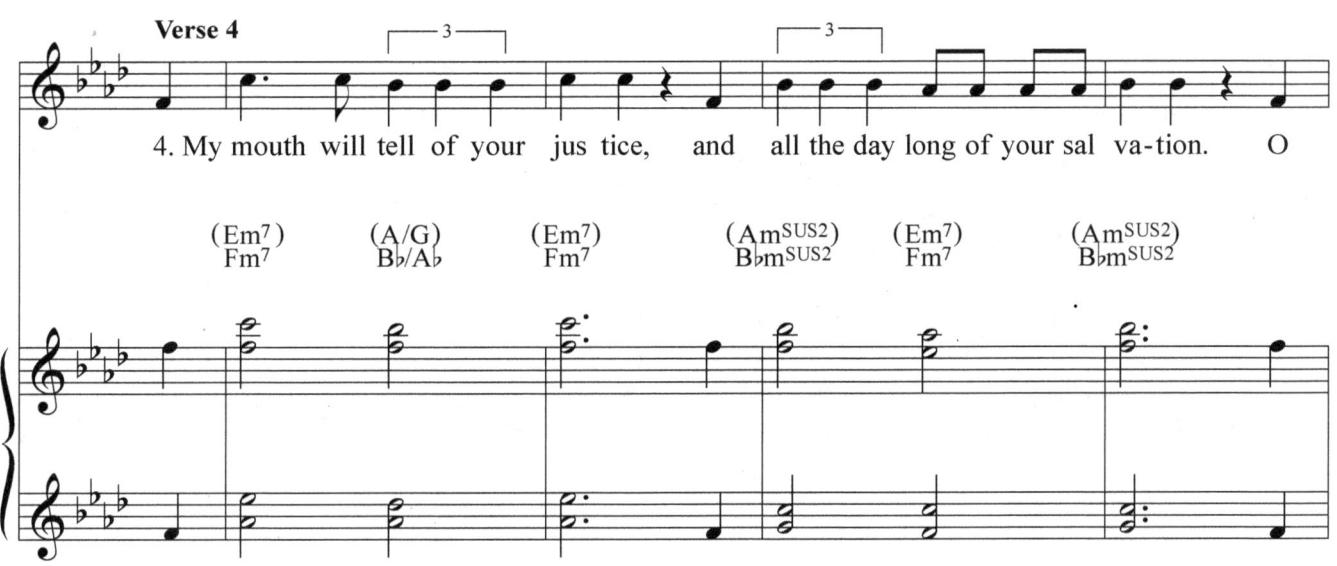

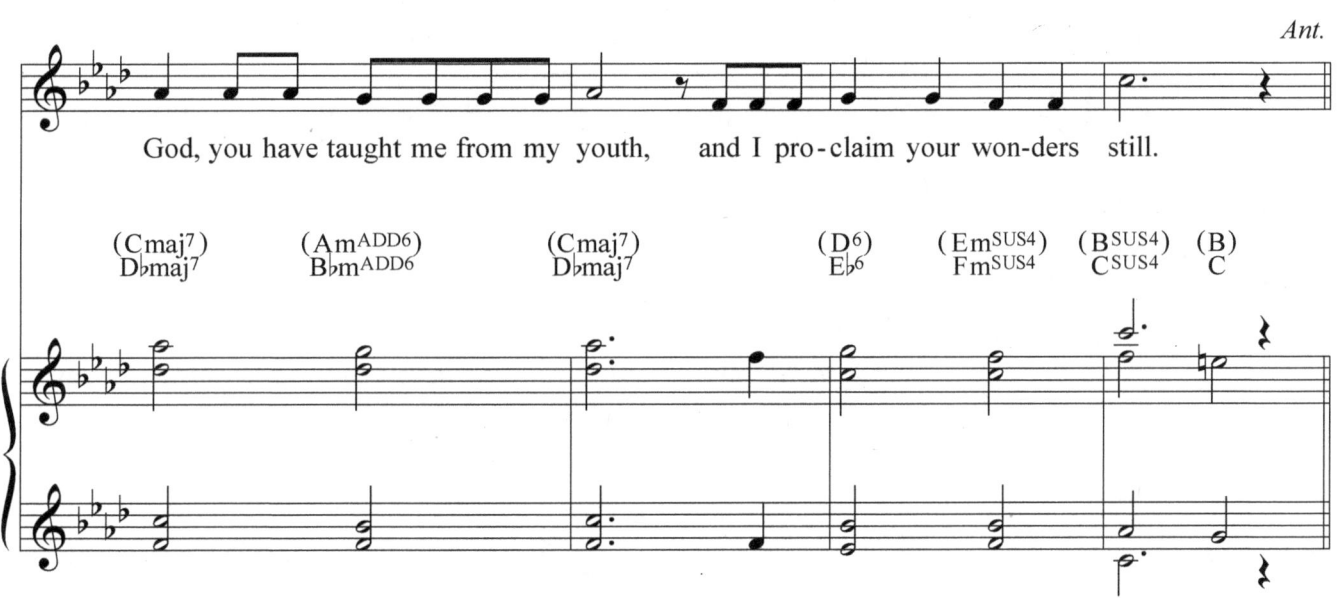

Psalm 138: In the Sight of the Angels
Fifth Sunday in Ordinary Time, Year C

Ps 138:1-2ab, 2cde-3, 4-5, 7c-8

Michael Joncas
Tone 5B: Individual Thanksgiving

Fifth Sunday in Ordinary Time, Year C

Fifth Sunday in Ordinary Time, Year C

Ant.

sing of the ways of the LORD, "How great is the glo-ry of the LORD!"

G⁶   F♯7   Bm   D   Em   Em⁷   A^SUS4   A

Verse 4

4. With your right hand you save me; the LORD will ac-com-plish this for me. O LORD, your

D   D/C♯   D^SUS2   D   Em⁷   Dmaj⁷   A^SUS4   A/G

Ant.

mer-ci-ful love is e-ter-nal; dis-card not the work of your hands.

G⁶   F♯7   Bm   D   Em   Em⁷   A^SUS4   A

Psalm 1: Blessed Are They
Sixth Sunday in Ordinary Time, Year C

Ps 1:1-2, 3, 4 and 6

Michael Joncas
Tone 8A: Wisdom Psalm 1

Sixth Sunday in Ordinary Time, Year C

Sixth Sunday in Ordinary Time, Year C

Sixth Sunday in Ordinary Time, Year C

Psalm 103: The Lord Is Kind
Seventh Sunday in Ordinary Time, Year C

Ps 103:1-2, 3-4, 8 and 10, 12-13

Michael Joncas
Tone 5B: Individual Thanksgiving

Seventh Sunday in Ordinary Time, Year C

Seventh Sunday in Ordinary Time, Year C

Verse 3

3. The LORD is com-pas-sion-ate and gra-cious, slow to an-ger and rich in

D   D/C♯   D^SUS2   D   Em^7   D/C♯

mer - cy. He does not treat us ac-cord-ing to our sins, nor re-

A^SUS4   A   Em^7   F♯^7   Bm   D/A

pay us ac-cor-ding to our faults.   *Ant.* **Verse 4**   4. As far as the east is from the west, so far from

G^6   Em^7   A^SUS4 A   D   D/C♯   D^SUS2 D

Seventh Sunday in Ordinary Time, Year C

us does he re-move our trans - gres-sions.   As a   fa - ther has com-pas-sion on his

child - ren,   the LORD's com - pas - sion is   on those who   fear him.

Psalm 92: Lord, It Is Good

Eighth Sunday in Ordinary Time, Year C

Ps 92:2-3, 13-14, 15-16

Michael Joncas
Tone 5A: Communal Thanksgiving

Antiphon

Proclamatory ♩ = 80

Harmony: Lord, it is good to give thanks to you, to give thanks to you.

Melody: Lord, it is good to give thanks to you, to give thanks to you.

Verse 1

1. It is good to give thanks to the LORD, to make mu-sic to your name, O

Eighth Sunday in Ordinary Time, Year C

Eighth Sunday in Ordinary Time, Year C

Eighth Sunday in Ordinary Time, Year C

up - right. In him, my rock, there is no wrong!

Psalm 117: Go Out to All the World
Ninth Sunday in Ordinary Time, Year C

Ps 117:1, 2

Michael Joncas
Tone 1B: Hymn of Praise,
Motivation from History or Torah

Ninth Sunday in Ordinary Time, Year C

Psalm 30: I Will Praise You, Lord
Tenth Sunday in Ordinary Time, Year C

Ps 30:2 and 4, 5-6, 11-12a and 13b

Michael Joncas
Tone 4C: Prayer for the Sick

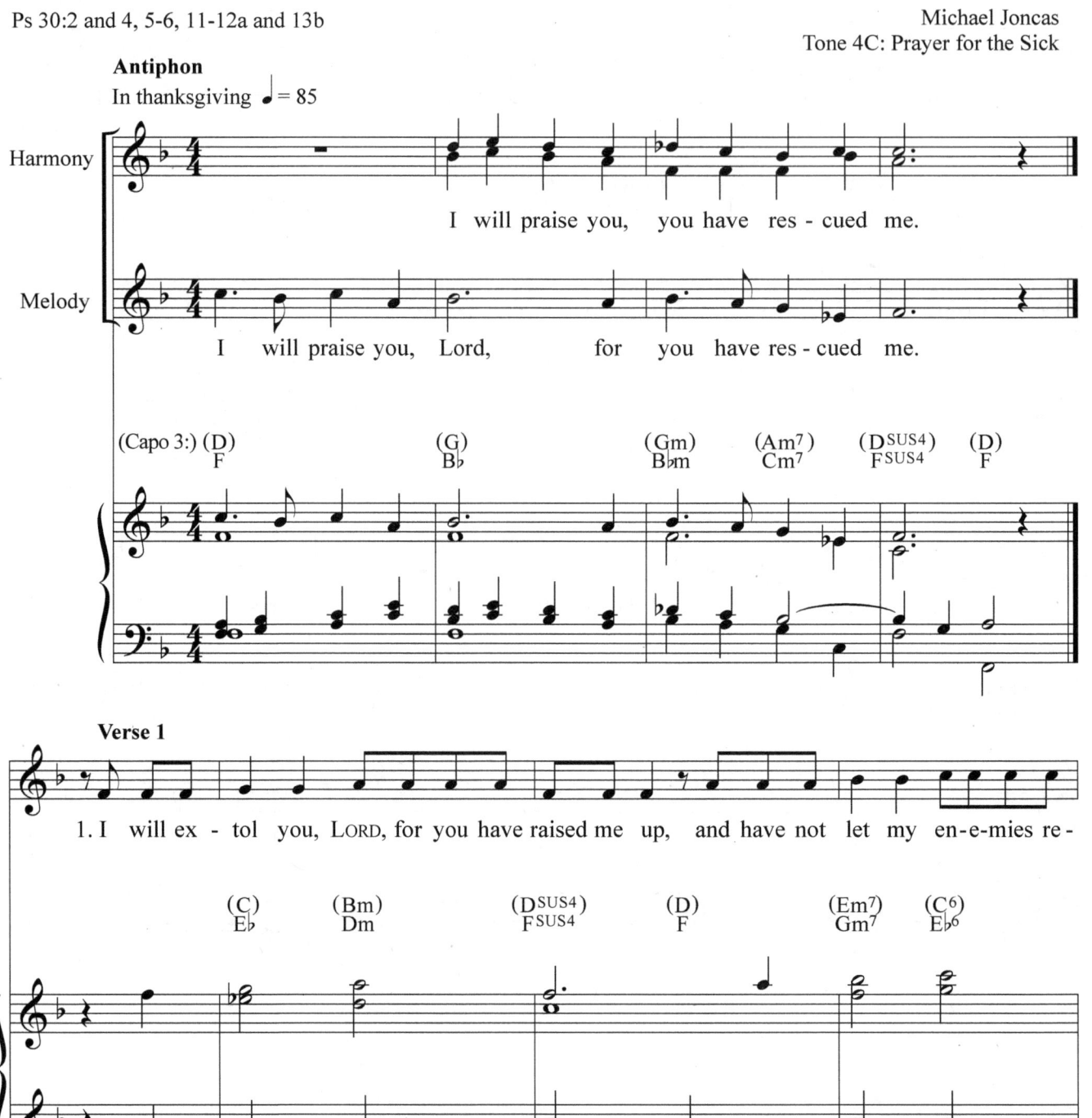

Tenth Sunday in Ordinary Time, Year C

Tenth Sunday in Ordinary Time, Year C

Psalm 32: Lord, Forgive the Wrong
Eleventh Sunday in Ordinary Time, Year C

Ps 32:1-2, 5, 7, 11

Michael Joncas
Tone 8A: Wisdom Psalm 1

Antiphon

Forthrightly ♩ = 80

Harmony: Lord, for-give, for - give the wrong I have done.

Melody: Lord, for- give, for - give the wrong I have done.

Verse 1

1. Blessed is he whose trans-gres-sion is for-giv-en, whose

Eleventh Sunday in Ordinary Time, Year C

Eleventh Sunday in Ordinary Time, Year C

Eleventh Sunday in Ordinary Time, Year C

Psalm 63: My Soul Is Thirsting for You
Twelfth Sunday in Ordinary Time, Year C

Ps 63:2, 3-4, 5-6, 8-9

Michael Joncas
Tone 4B: Individual Lament

Twelfth Sunday in Ordinary Time, Year C

Twelfth Sunday in Ordinary Time, Year C

Verse 3

3. I will bless you all my life; in your name I will lift up my hands. My

soul shall be filled as with a ban-quet; with joy-ful lips, my mouth shall praise you.

Ant.

Verse 4

4. For you have been my strength; in the shad-ow of your wings I re - joice. My

Twelfth Sunday in Ordinary Time, Year C

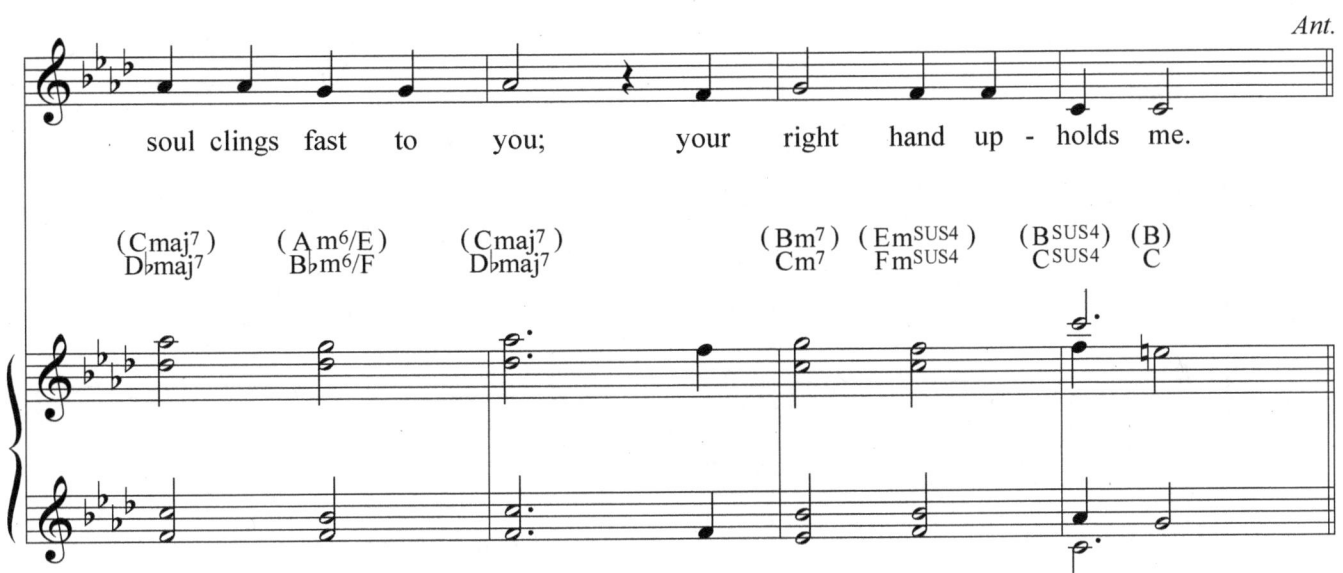

Psalm 16: You Are My Inheritance
Thirteenth Sunday in Ordinary Time, Year C

Ps 16:1-2a and 5, 7-8, 9-10, 11

Michael Joncas
Tone 4C: Prayer for the Sick

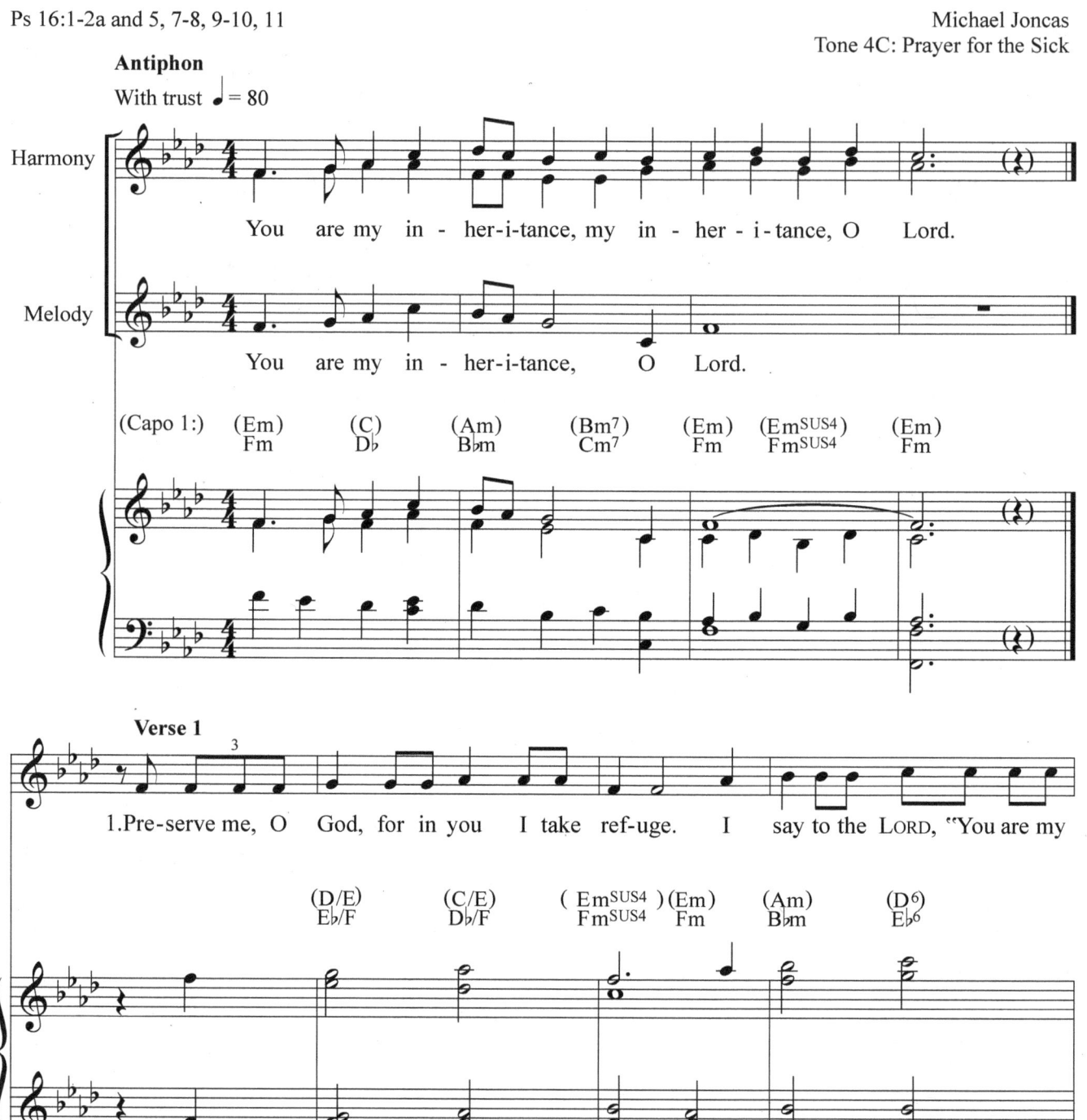

Thirteenth Sunday in Ordinary Time, Year C

Psalm 66: Let All the Earth
Fourteenth Sunday in Ordinary Time, Year C

Ps 66:1-3a, 4-5, 6-7a, 16 and 20

Michael Joncas
Tone 5B: Individual Thanksgiving

Fourteenth Sunday in Ordinary Time, Year C

ren-der him glo-rious praise.   Say to God, "How won-drous your deeds!"

Verse 2

2. "Be - fore you all the earth shall bow down,   shall sing to you, sing to your name!"

Come   and see the works of God;   his won-drous deeds a-mong the chil-dren of Ad-am.

Fourteenth Sunday in Ordinary Time, Year C

Verse 3

3. He turned the sea in-to dry land; they passed through the riv-er on foot. Let our

D   D/C♯   D^SUS2   D   Em^7   Dmaj^7   A^SUS4   A

Ant.

joy, then, be in him; he rules for-ev-er by his might.

G^6   F♯^7   Bm   D   Em   Em^7   A^SUS4   A

Verse 4

4. Come and hear, all who fear God; I will tell what he did for my

D   D/C♯   D^SUS2   D   Em^7   Dmaj^7

Fourteenth Sunday in Ordinary Time, Year C

soul.   Blest be God, who did not   re - ject my   prayer,   nor with -

hold from me   his   mer - ci - ful   love.

Psalm 69: Turn to the Lord

Fifteenth Sunday in Ordinary Time, Year C, first setting

Ps 69:14 and 17, 30-31, 33-34, 36ab and 37

Michael Joncas
Tone 4B: Individual Lament

Turn, O turn to the Lord and you live.

Turn to the Lord in your need, and you will live.

1. I pray to you, O Lord, at an ac-cept-a-ble time. In

Fifteenth Sunday in Ordinary Time, Year C, first setting

Fifteenth Sunday in Ordinary Time, Year C, first setting

Fifteenth Sunday in Ordinary Time, Year C, first setting

need-y,   and does not spurn his own in their chains.   4. For   God will bring sal-

va-tion   to   Zi - on,   and re - build the ci-ties of Ju-dah.   The   child-ren of his

ser-vants shall in - her-it it;   those who love   his name shall   dwell there.

Psalm 19: Lord, You Have the Words
Fifteenth Sunday in Ordinary Time, Year C, second setting

Ps 19:8, 9, 10, 11

Michael Joncas
Tone 8B: Wisdom Psalm 2

Antiphon

Simply ♩ = 90

Your words, O Lord, are Spir-it and life.

Your words, O Lord, are Spir - it and life.

Verse 1

1. The law of the LORD is per - fect; it re - vives the soul. The de-

Fifteenth Sunday in Ordinary Time, Year C, second setting

Fifteenth Sunday in Ordinary Time, Year C, second setting

Fifteenth Sunday in Ordinary Time, Year C, second setting

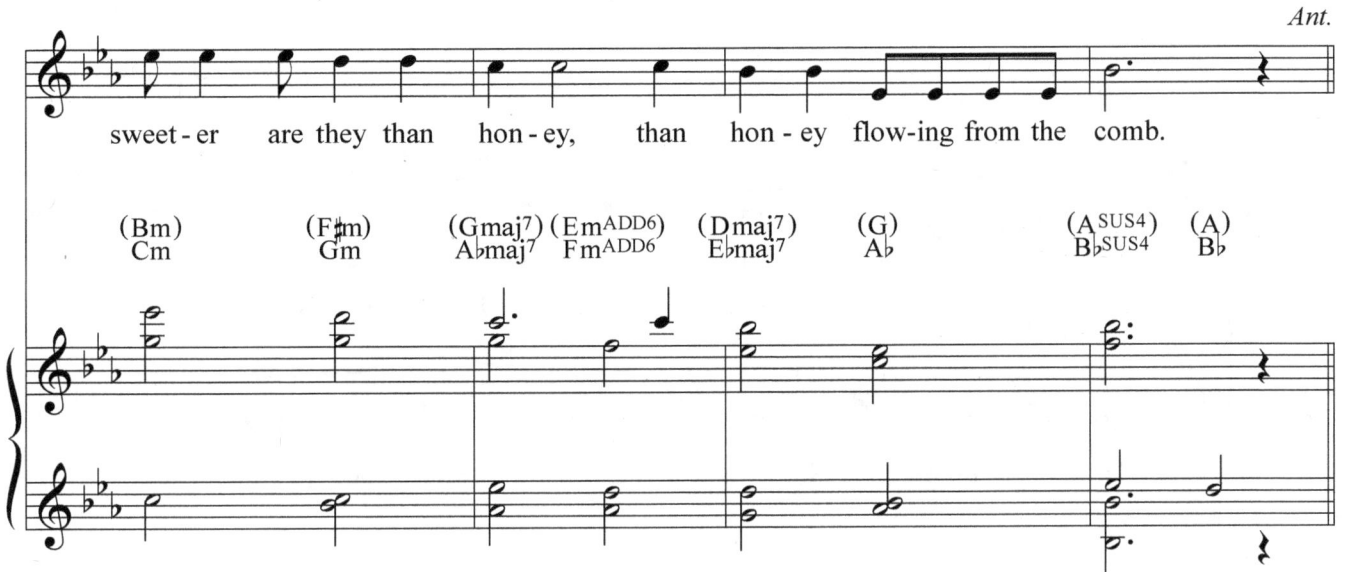

Ant.

sweet-er are they than hon-ey, than hon-ey flow-ing from the comb.

Psalm 15: The One Who Does Justice
Sixteenth Sunday in Ordinary Time, Year C

Ps 15:2-3, 3-4, 5

Michael Joncas
Tone 1D: Processional

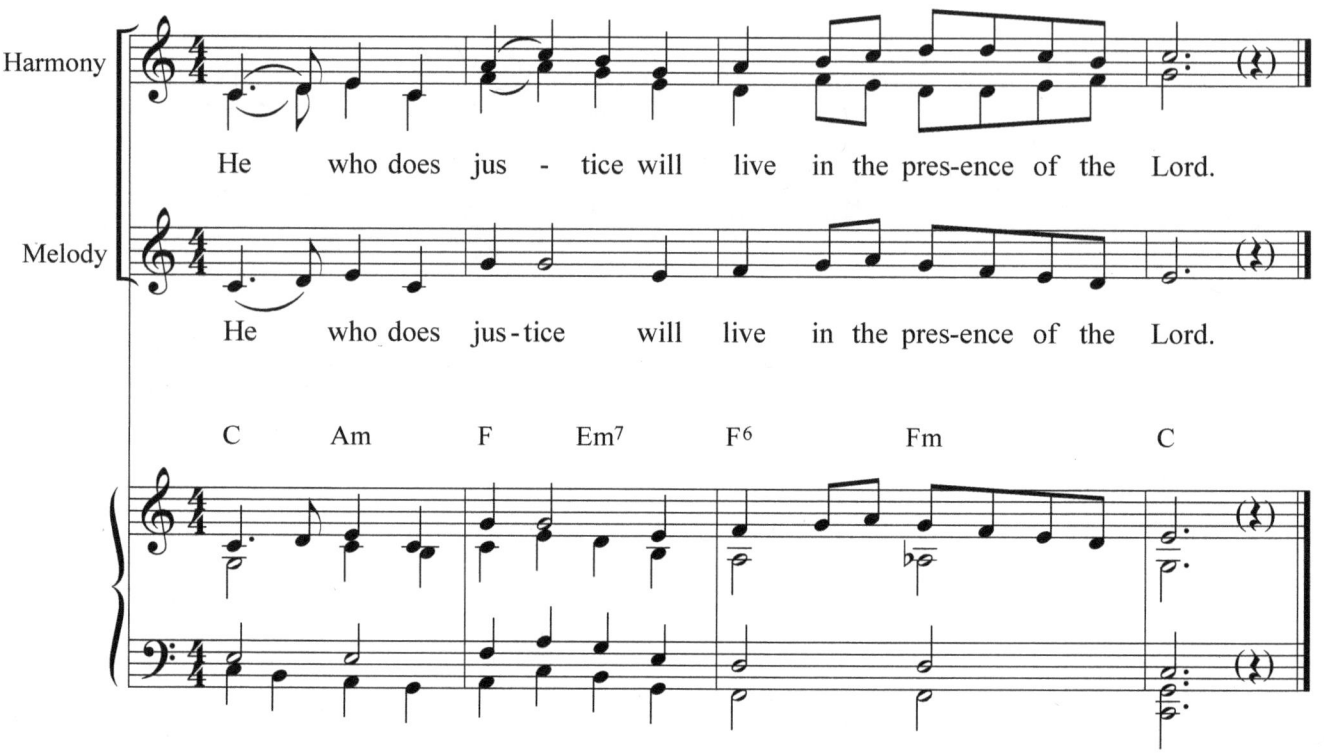

Verse 1

Sixteenth Sunday in Ordinary Time, Year C

Sixteenth Sunday in Ordinary Time, Year C

Psalm 138: Lord, on the Day I Called for Help
Seventeenth Sunday in Ordinary Time, Year C

Ps 138:1-2ab, 2cde-3, 6-7ab, 7c-8

Michael Joncas
Tone 5B: Individual Thanksgiving

Seventeenth Sunday in Ordinary Time, Year C

heard the words of my mouth.   In the pres-ence of the an-gels I   praise you.   I bow

Em7   Dmaj7   A^SUS4   A/G   G6   F#7   Bm   D

Ant.

down   toward your ho - ly   tem - ple.   I give thanks   to your   name.

A   E7   A^SUS4   A/G   Em   Em7   A^SUS4   A

Verse 2

2. I give thanks for your mer-ci-ful love and your faith-ful-ness;   for   you have ex-alt-ed ov-er

D   D/C#   D^SUS2   D   Em7   Dmaj7

Seventeenth Sunday in Ordinary Time, Year C

Psalm 90: If Today You Hear His Voice
Eighteenth Sunday in Ordinary Time, Year C

Ps 90:3-4, 5-6, 12-13, 14 and 17

Michael Joncas
Tone 4A: Community Lament

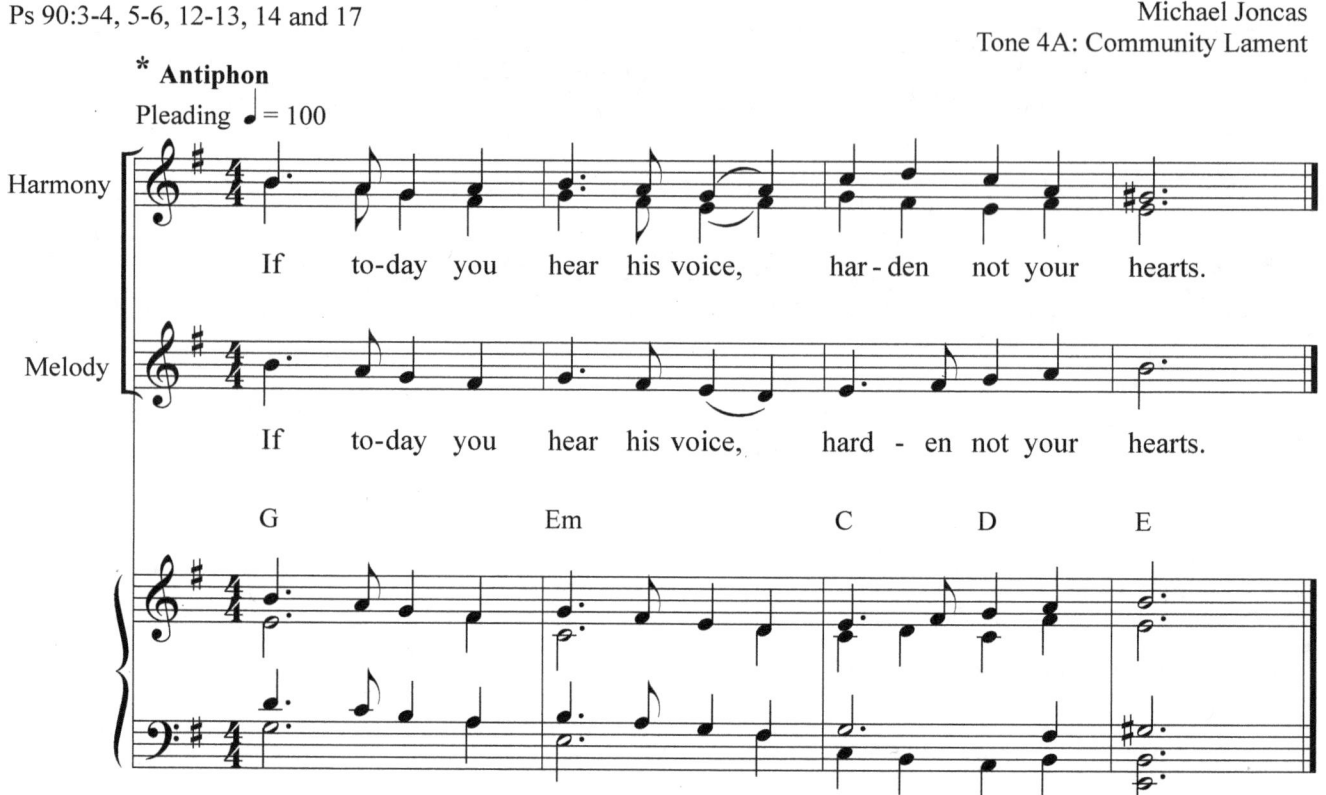

*** Note:**

In the 1969 Roman Lectionary, the 18th Sunday in Ordinary Time originally specified Psalm **95** with the response or antiphon *If today you hear his voice,* as above. The revised 1981 Roman Lectionary changed this to Psalm **90**, which fits better thematically.

However, the compilers of the U.S. 1981 Lectionary overlooked the response, which should also have been changed, and so the 18th Sunday now has Psalm 90 for the verses but still has the original response from Psalm 95, *If today you hear his voice,* which no longer fits the current psalm.

The correct response, as in the Roman Lectionary, should be the same as for the 23rd Sunday in Ordinary Time, five weeks later, which also specifies Psalm 90. On the following page we reproduce Father Joncas's antiphon for this day for those who wish to make this choice on the 18th Sunday as well.

* **Antiphon** *(from 23rd Sunday in Ordinary Time, Year C—see note on previous page)*

Pleading ♩ = 100

Eighteenth Sunday in Ordinary Time, Year C

Eighteenth Sunday in Ordinary Time, Year C

Psalm 33: Blessed the People

Nineteenth Sunday in Ordinary Time, Year C

Ps 33:1 and 12, 18-19, 20 and 22

Michael Joncas
Tone 1B: Hymn of Praise,
Motivation from History or Torah

Antiphon

With awe ♩ = 80

Harmony

Bless-ed the peo-ple the Lord has cho-sen, cho-sen to be his own.

Melody

Bless-ed the peo-ple the Lord has cho-sen, cho-sen to be his own.

(Capo 3:) (D) (G) (Gm) (D) (G) (C) (Am⁷) (D)
F Bb Bbm F Bb Eb Cm⁷ F

Verse 1

1. Ring out your joy to the LORD, all you just; for praise is fit-ting from the

(D) (C/D) (Bm) (D) (Em) (D)
F F/Eb Dm F Gm F

Nineteenth Sunday in Ordinary Time, Year C

Nineteenth Sunday in Ordinary Time, Year C

Verse 3

3. Our soul is wait-ing for the LORD. He is our help and our shield. May your mer-ci-ful love be up-on us, as we hope in you, O LORD.

Ant.

Psalm 40: Lord, Come to My Aid
Twentieth Sunday in Ordinary Time, Year C

Ps 40 (39):2, 3, 4, 18

Michael Joncas
Tone 5B: Individual Thanksgiving

Antiphon
With thanksgiving ♩ = 95

Harmony: Lord, Lord, come to my aid!

Melody: Lord, Lord, come to my aid!

D   Em⁷   F♯m⁷   G   D^SUS4 D

Verse 1

1. I wait-ed, I wait-ed for the LORD, and he stooped down to me; he

D   D/C♯   D^SUS2   D   Em   Em⁷   A^SUS4   A

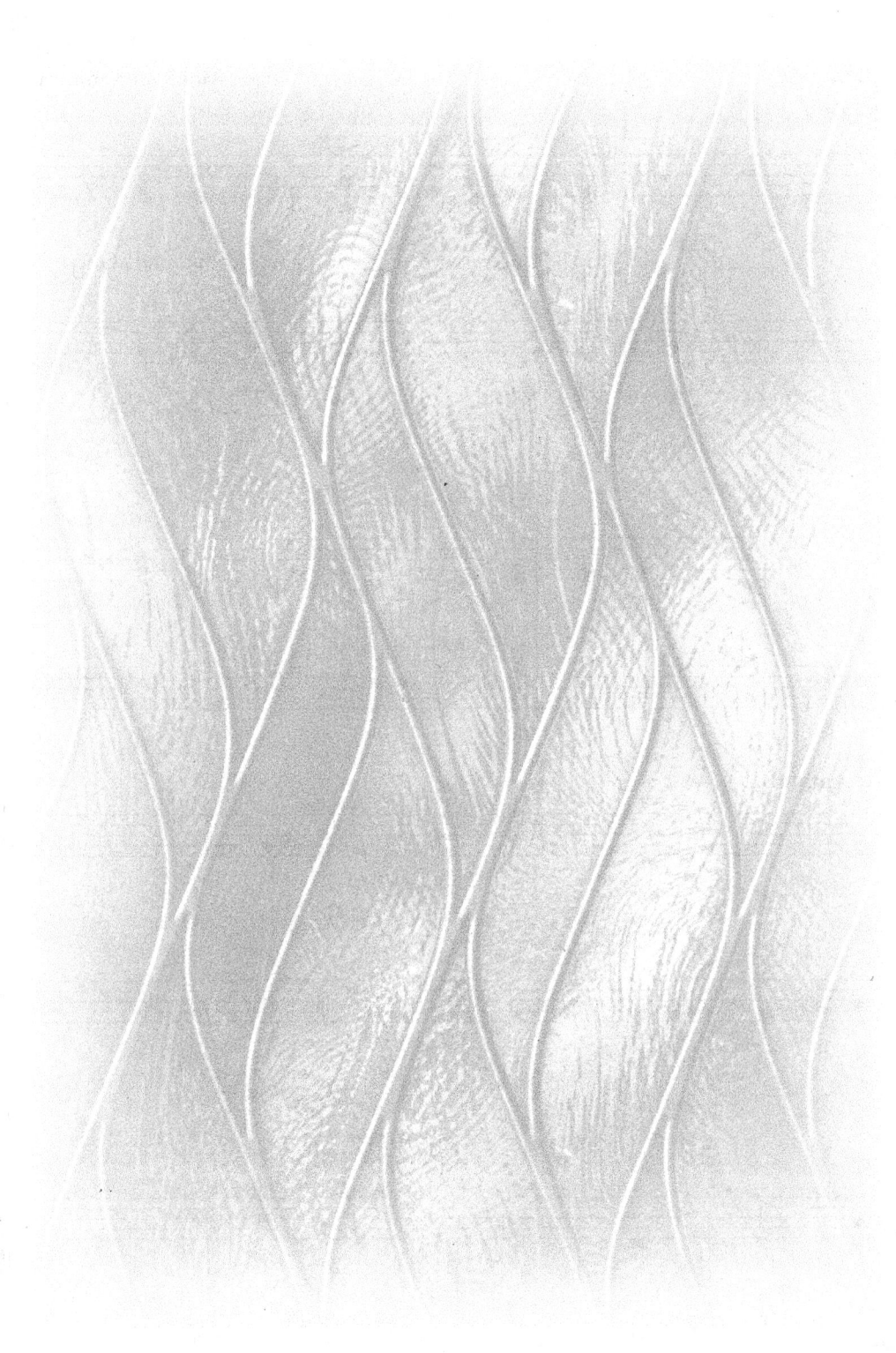

Psalm 117: Go Out to All the World
Twenty-First Sunday in Ordinary Time, Year C

Ps 117:1, 2

Michael Joncas
Tone 1B: Hymn of Praise,
Motivation from History or Torah

Twenty-First Sunday in Ordinary Time, Year C

Psalm 68: God in Your Goodness
Twenty-Second Sunday in Ordinary Time, Year C

Ps 68:4-5ac, 6-7ab, 10-11

Michael Joncas
Tone 1B: Hymn of Praise, Motivation from History or Torah

Twenty-Second Sunday in Ordinary Time, Year C

Twenty-Second Sunday in Ordinary Time, Year C

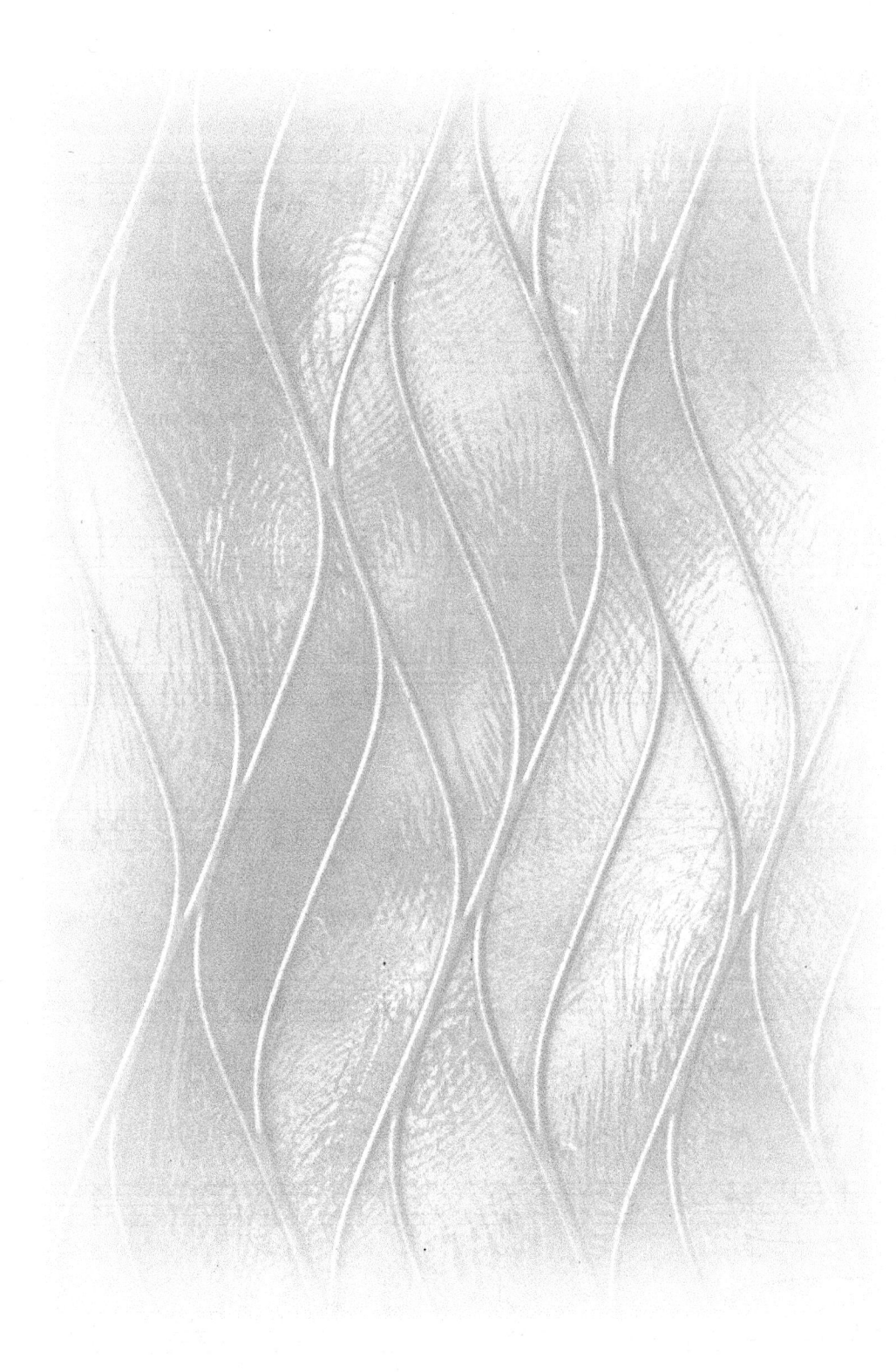

Psalm 90: In Every Age, O Lord
Twenty-Third Sunday in Ordinary Time, Year C

Ps 90:3-4, 5-6, 12-13, 14 and 17

Michael Joncas
Tone 4A: Community Lament

Twenty-Third Sunday in Ordinary Time, Year C

Twenty-Third Sunday in Ordinary Time, Year C

Twenty-Third Sunday in Ordinary Time, Year C

Psalm 51: I Will Rise
Twenty-Fourth Sunday in Ordinary Time, Year C

Ps 51:3-4, 12-13, 17 and 19

Michael Joncas
Tone 4B: Individual Lament

Twenty-Fourth Sunday in Ordinary Time, Year C

Twenty-Fourth Sunday in Ordinary Time, Year C

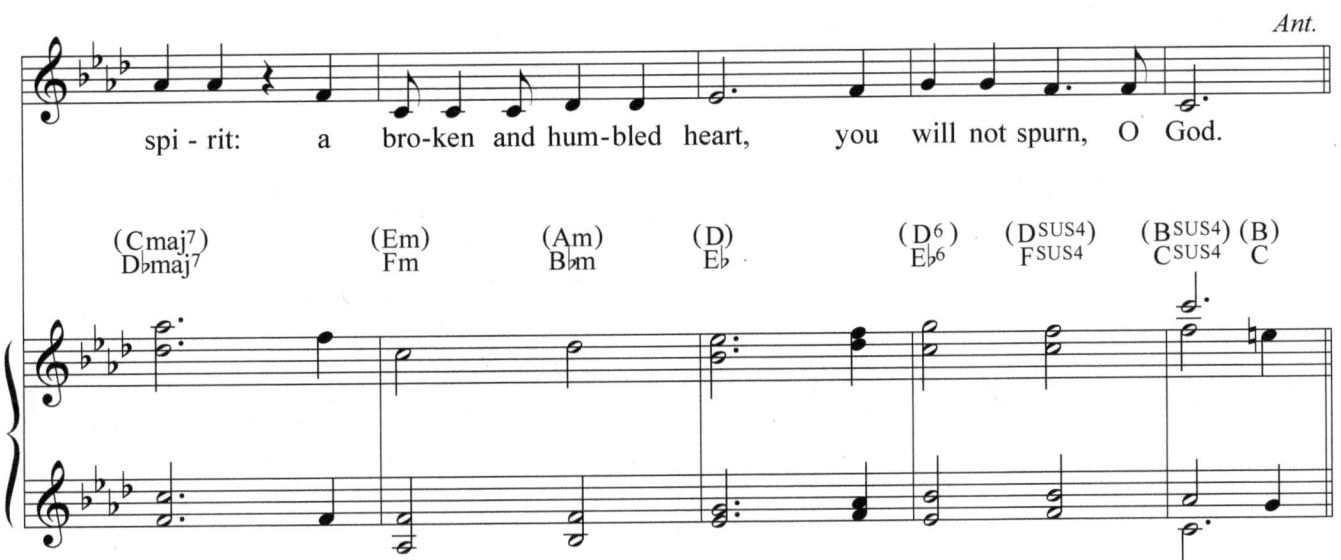

Psalm 113: Praise the Lord
Twenty-Fifth Sunday in Ordinary Time, Year C

Ps 113:1-2, 4-6, 7-8

Michael Joncas
Tone 1B: Hymn of Praise, Motivation from History or Torah

Twenty-Fifth Sunday in Ordinary Time, Year C

Twenty-Fifth Sunday in Ordinary Time, Year C

Twenty-Fifth Sunday in Ordinary Time, Year C

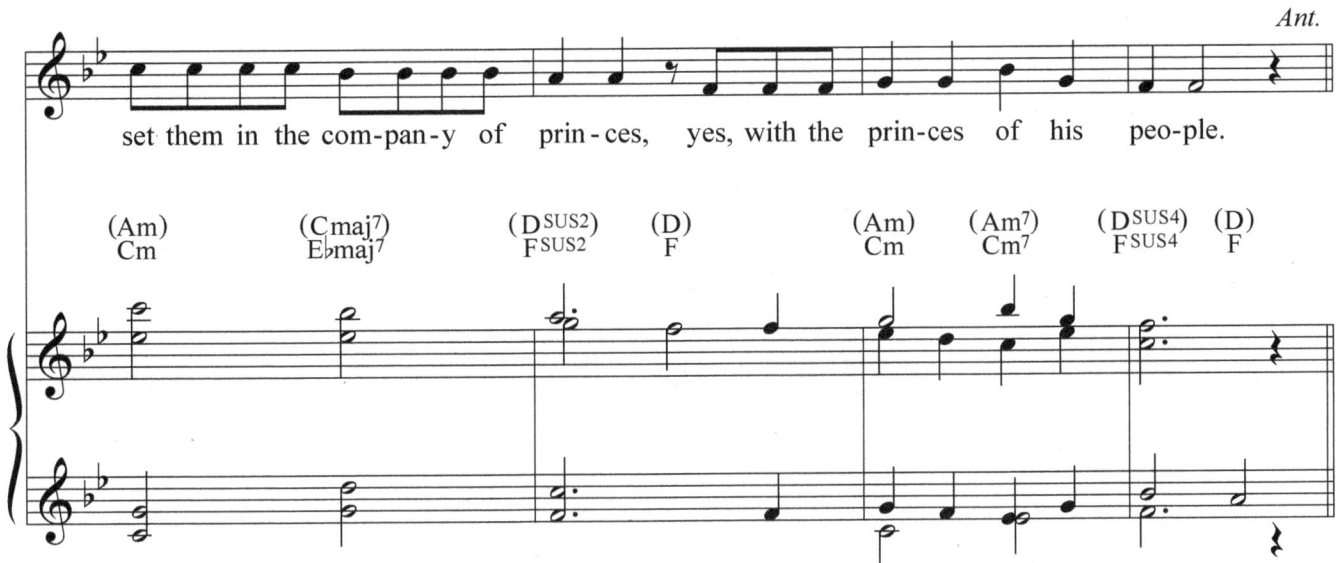

Psalm 146: Praise the Lord, My Soul!
Twenty-Sixth Sunday in Ordinary Time, Year C

Ps 146:6c-7, 8-9a, 9bc-10

Michael Joncas
Tone 1B: Hymn of Praise,
Motivation from History or Torah

Antiphon
With intensity ♩ = 90

Harmony: Praise the Lord, my soul! O praise the Lord, my soul!

Melody: Praise the Lord, my soul! Praise the Lord, my soul!

(Capo 3:) (G)/B♭ (Bm)/Dm (C)/E♭ (G)/B♭ (C)/E♭ (Am⁷)/Cm⁷ (D)/F (G)/B♭

Alternate Antiphon

Al-le-lu-ia, al-le-lu-ia, al-le-lu-ia!

Al-le-lu-ia, al-le-lu-ia, al-le-lu-ia!

(G)/B♭ (Bm)/Dm (C)/E♭ (G)/B♭ (C)/E♭ (A⁷)/Cm⁷ (D)/F (G)/B♭

Twenty-Sixth Sunday in Ordinary Time, Year C

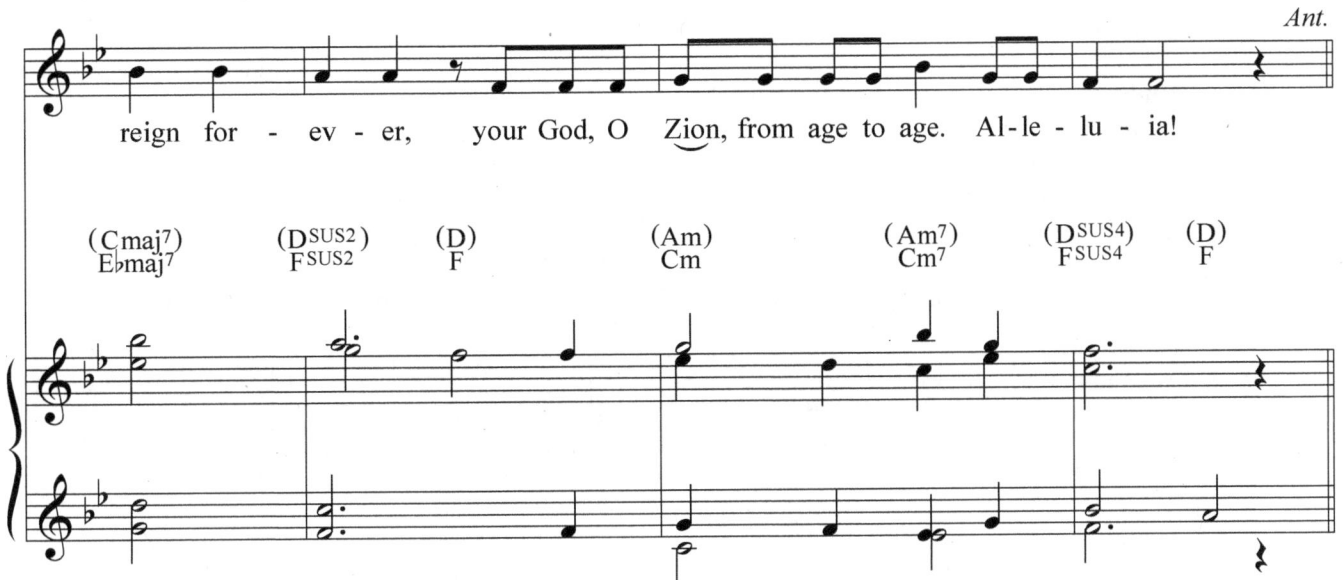

Psalm 95: If Today You Hear His Voice
Twenty-Seventh Sunday in Ordinary Time, Year C

Ps 95:1-2, 6-7ab, 7c-9

Michael Joncas
Tone 1D: Processional

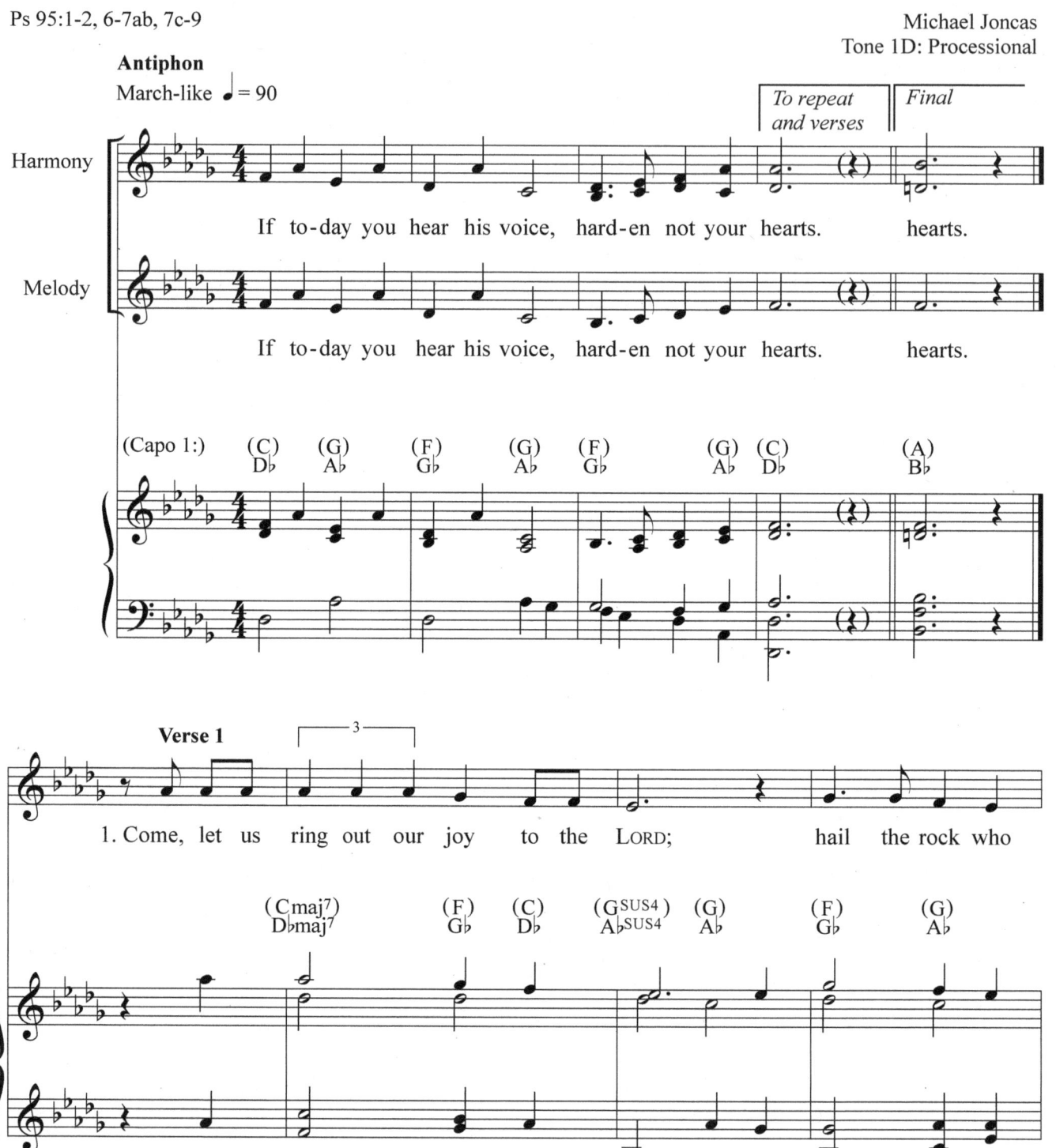

Twenty-Seventh Sunday in Ordinary Time, Year C

fore-bears put me to the test; when they tried me, though they saw my work."

Psalm 98: The Lord Has Revealed
Twenty-Eighth Sunday in Ordinary Time, Year C

Ps 98:1, 2-3ab, 3cd-4

Michael Joncas
Tone 1E: Hymn of Praise to YHWH as King

Twenty-Eighth Sunday in Ordinary Time, Year C

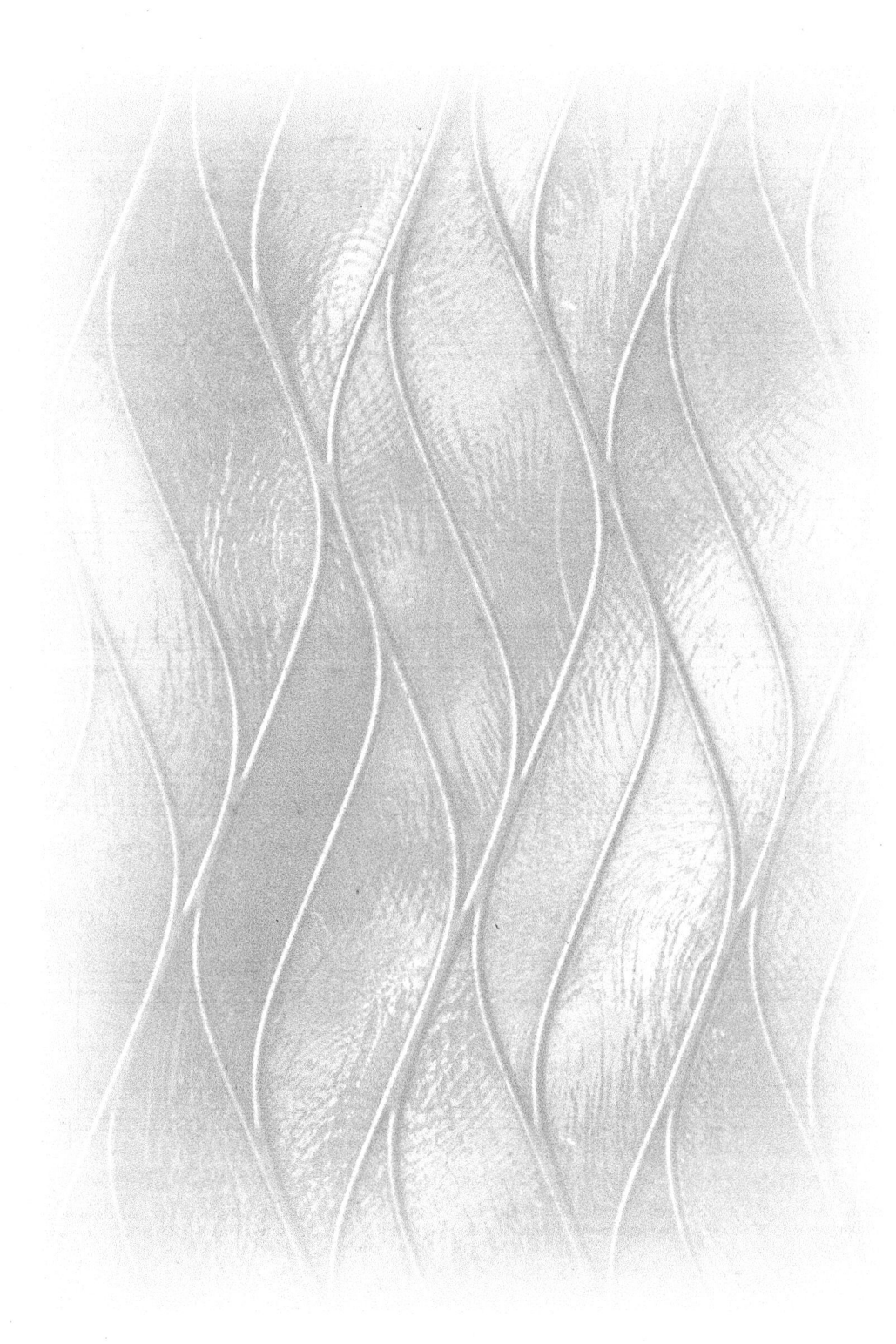

Psalm 121: Our Help Is from the Lord

Twenty-Ninth Sunday in Ordinary Time, Year C

Ps 121(120):1-2, 3-4, 5-6, 7-8

Michael Joncas
Tone 6: Psalm of Confidence

Twenty-Ninth Sunday in Ordinary Time, Year C

Ant.

LORD will guard your go - ing and com - ing, both now and for - ev - er.

Am   F   Dm⁷   Am   C   G^{SUS4} G

Psalm 34: The Lord Hears the Cry
Thirtieth Sunday in Ordinary Time, Year C

Ps 34:2-3, 17-18, 19 and 23

Michael Joncas
Tone 8A: Wisdom Psalm 1

Antiphon

With delight ♩ = 90

Harmony: The Lord hears the cry of the poor.

Melody: The Lord hears the cry, the cry of the poor.

D   Bm   Em   Gmaj⁷   A⁷   D

Verse 1

1. I will bless the LORD at all times, praise of him is al-ways in my

D   A   Bm   D   Em⁷   D

Thirtieth Sunday in Ordinary Time, Year C

Thirtieth Sunday in Ordinary Time, Year C

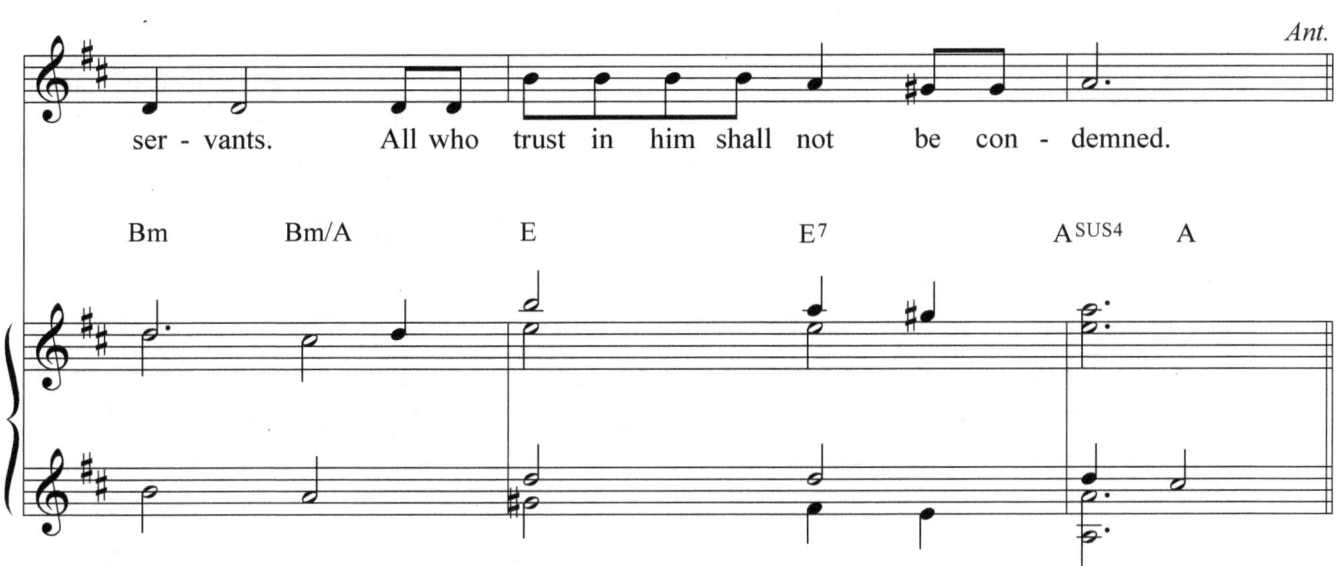

Psalm 145: I Will Praise Your Name For Ever
Thirty-First Sunday in Ordinary Time, Year C

Ps 145:1-2, 8-9, 10-11, 13cd-14

Michael Joncas
Tone 1B: Hymn of Praise,
Motivation from History or Torah

Thirty-First Sunday in Ordinary Time, Year C

Thirty-First Sunday in Ordinary Time, Year C

Verse 4

4. The LORD is faith-ful in all his words, and ho-ly in all his deeds. The LORD sup-

ports all who fall, and rais-es up all who are bowed down.

Psalm 17: Lord, When Your Glory Appears
Thirty-Second Sunday in Ordinary Time, Year C

Ps 17:1, 5-6, 8 and 15

Michael Joncas
Tone 4B: Individual Lament

Antiphon

Trustingly ♩ = 80

Harmony: Lord, Lord, when your glo-ry ap-pears, my joy will be full.

Melody: Lord, Lord, when your glo-ry ap-pears, my joy will be full.

Verse 1

1. O LORD, hear a cause that is just, pay heed to my cry.

Psalm 98: The Lord Comes to Rule the Earth

Thirty-Third Sunday in Ordinary Time, Year C

Ps 98:5-6, 7-8, 9

Michael Joncas
Tone 1E: Hymn of Praise to YHWH as King

Thirty-Third Sunday in Ordinary Time, Year C

Thirty-Third Sunday in Ordinary Time, Year C

Thirty-Third Sunday in Ordinary Time, Year C

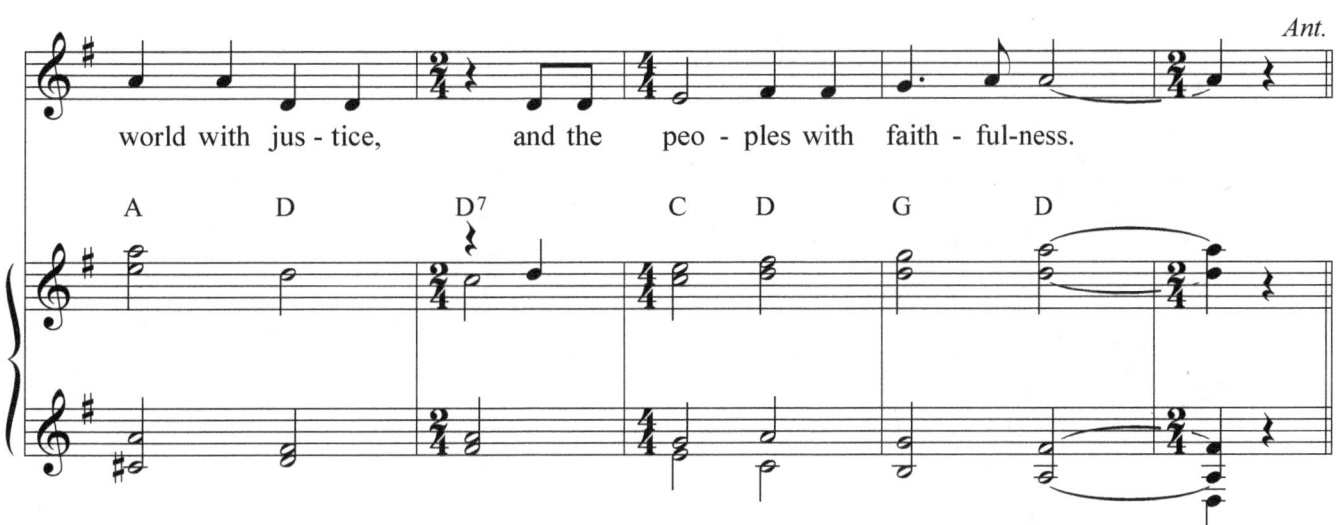

Psalm 122: Let Us Go Rejoicing

Solemnity of Christ the King/Thirty-Fourth Sunday in Ordinary Time, Year C

Ps 122:1-2, 3-4ab, 4cd-5

Michael Joncas
Tone 1C: Song of Zion

Solemnity of Christ the King/Thirty-Fourth Sunday in Ordinary Time, Year C

Solemnity of Christ the King/Thirty-Fourth Sunday in Ordinary Time, Year C